Christ Frees and Unites

By Martin J. Heinecken

THE KNUBEL-MILLER LECTURES—1957

Christ Frees and Unites

By

Martin J. Heinecken

BOARD OF PUBLICATION
OF THE UNITED LUTHERAN CHURCH IN AMERICA
PHILADELPHIA

Library of Congress Catalog
Card Number 57-11301

Printed in U.S.A.

Table of Contents

Foreword

The theme "Christ Frees and Unites" was selected for the 1957 Lutheran World Assembly. Its choice grew out of the conviction that in the present movements toward unity a peculiar "kairos," a crucial moment of responsibility and opportunity, confronts the Lutheran Church. What will the church of the Reformation declare to be essential to the true unity of the church? The answer that speaks from the heart of the Reformation is that "the way to the center is the way to unity." The way to unity is the way of freedom in Christ. Those who are free men in Christ are also one in Christ.

A preliminary drafting of the topics to be treated at the Lutheran World Assembly in Minneapolis, August 16-25, 1957, includes: 1. The Meaning of Freedom in Christ; 2. Christian Freedom and the Unity of the Church; 3. Loyalty and Freedom in the Reformation of the Church; 4. The Freedom and Unity of the Church in Its Service to the World; and 5. The Freedom and Unity of the Church in the Light of the Kingdom to Come.

The Knubel-Miller Lectures for 1957 deal with certain aspects of these topics as they apply particularly to the American scene. They mean to contribute to our own Lutheran unity, to make clear our witness in the ecumenical church, and also to speak a liberating and unifying word to the non-Christian people of the world in their restless search for freedom and unity.

March 1957 — MARTIN J. HEINECKEN

I

Toward Unity in the Church

My task in this volume has been cut out for me; namely, to discuss the theme of the Lutheran World Assembly (Minneapolis, 1957), which is "Christ Frees and Unites." In this first chapter I want to try to set the stage for the succeeding ones by reviewing briefly some of the significant movements toward unity and the Lutheran Church's part in them, giving the reasons for the choice of the theme, and stating how, in my opinion, the discussions on the theme should fit into this picture. It is my hope that thereby a threefold purpose may be fulfilled: 1) to contribute to our Lutheran unity, 2) to make clear our witness in the ecumenical church, 3) to set the liberating and uniting gospel clearly before the people of the world in their restless search for freedom and unity.

The choice of the theme of "unity" was natural in the light of the movements toward unity everywhere in the churches today, which issue not only out of the growing oneness of the world and a pragmatic concern to present a united front to a totalitarian foe, but out of a mood of deep and genuine repentance for a disunited church which stands in contradiction to the "one, holy, catholic, apostolic church."[1] If the Lutheran Church is to be true to her heritage she cannot dissociate herself from wholehearted participation in the "ecumenical movement" and members of the LWF

[1] See W. A. Visser 't Hooft: "The Issues to be Faced at Evanston," The *Chicago Theological Seminary Register,* January, 1954, p. 7.

[2] See Article III, Nature and Purpose, 2d: "To foster participation in ecumenical movements."

are in fact pledged to such participation by its constitution.[2] No apologies therefore are needed for turning to the discussion of unity at this time. But the peculiar combination of "freedom and unity," which strikes many as getting off on the wrong foot, does need some justification. It is precisely this combination which I sincerely believe presented itself providentially to those charged with the responsibility of choosing a theme, and I do not mean thereby to identify the guidance of the Holy Spirit with the compromises at which a weary and wrangling committee finally arrived.

At the first meeting of the enlarged theological commission[3] Bishop Hanns Lilje, president of the LWF, spoke of a *kairos* confronting the Lutheran Church. If this is not to be interpreted as a presumption we must keep in mind the biblical conception of the *kairos,* the "fulness of time," the crucial, decisive moment of responsibility, opportunity, and judgment. For the Christian there is the one central, absolutely decisive *kairos,* that one "moment" which marks the turning point and, therefore, the center of all history, because in it God acted decisively and victoriously for the redemption of the world and at the same time also as judgment upon it. But there are also other *kairoi* which for the individuals involved in them are equally crucial and decisive. We are not speaking now, of course, of the possible stock-market cleaning a man might have made if only he had taken the right tip or the play the quarterback might have called in the championship game to tip the scales from defeat to victory. We are speaking of those crucial turning points which are the counterparts in the lives of individuals or that one decisive turning point in the history of the world from defeat to victory, enslavement to freedom, fragmentization to unity.

So there are also given to the church from time to time peculiar, crucial moments of responsibility and opportunity, when the times are ripe. If responded to in faith they will result in a fresh outpouring of God's Spirit, the winning of many for the kingdom of God and a strengthening of the saving structures of grace in the world.

[3] Hamburg, February, 1955.

The Reformation, we who are of the Reformation believe, was such a time when a concatenation of factors constituted a *kairos* which was responded to and resulted in a new birth of true freedom and a purging of the church from falsehood and man-made machinations.

Is it now a presumption for the president of the LWF to say that at present a peculiar *kairos* confronts particularly the Lutheran Church, which is the direct heir of the initial reform movement? Is it a presumption for him to suggest that what is said must be said so clearly and strikingly that people will nudge themselves in the street and say, "Did you hear what those Lutherans are saying?"

It was Luther, because he was held captive in conscience by the Word of God and would not budge from the center in Christ, who was responsible for the breach with Rome. Will it be the heirs of Luther who point the way back to unity by pointing to that center as unequivocally as he did? Lutherans now constitute the largest single Protestant denomination (*ca.* 70,000,000), spread over the entire world and all bound together by the confession to which the original Reformers subscribed. Does this mean bondage to a dead past or is it a real charter of liberty? What has the church of the Reformation to say at a time like this?

Surely it is not a proud presumption to suggest that a tremendous responsibility is placed upon the Lutheran Church at this time. It called not for smug satisfaction with what we regard as our possession. The gospel is never any man's secure possession, but always only the renewed gift of God. So this *kairos* calls rather for thorough self-examination in the light of that Word of God to which alone the Reformers were subservient. It calls for a real humbling of the self under the Lord of the church and a willingness to be persuaded by sound reasoning and the Word of God and to be in conscience bound by nothing other than that Word itself. We are under a Lord whose present guidance we must be willing to follow step for step. We are not to hold before us an ideal pattern of the church of the future fashioned after our fancy and then expect God to be on our side to help us in its realization. This is paganism, not Christianity. The fact that there is given to the Lutheran Church a *kairos* is by no means to be an occasion for pride. If this were taken to mean that we are chosen by God, because of our heritage, to speak the decisive word to the world at this time, I would be the last to want to affirm this. It means rather that here there is an opportunity, and whether or not we seize it, whether or not we become the instruments in God's hands to speak a decisive word at this time, still remains to be seen. A *kairos* is always also a moment of judgment. It depends on how humble we are, how open to the guidance of the Spirit, how seriously we examine ourselves, how receptive really to hear the Word and not just to talk about the church but to *be* the church.

Bishop Anders Nygren's words prior to Hannover, 1952, were clear: "When the Lutheran Churches gather for their World Assembly, this must needs be a *theological event* . . . . It is the first and foremost task of the Lutheran Church to deal with matters of theology — in the profoundest sense of that term. (For) the real purpose of theology is to help man in attaining the core of the gospel message . . . ." It is "from a deepened understanding of the gospel that the Reformation and the Lutheran Church have sprung. Therefore an ever deepening theological understanding of the gospel must remain the basis of its continued existence as a church."[4] It is not out of smug confessionalism that we are to speak—"No church . . . has the right to cultivate distinctive doctrines of its own. No church has permission to declare: in our group we are mainly interested in this or that particular doctrine and we push all other phases of the Christian faith into the background. No church has the right to say: we follow St. Paul and do not care about the rest of the New Testament . . . . There

[4] Quoted by E. Theodore Bachmann in *Epic of Faith* (New York: National Lutheran Council, 1952), pp. 27, 28.

is only one gospel. The church has the duty to proclaim the gospel, the whole gospel and nothing but the gospel . . . ." The purpose is "*not to reiterate what the Reformers said, but to rethink our gospel, the one and only gospel, the whole gospel; to study it anew, possibly from a new point of approach and to express it in the terms of today.*"[5] Therefore Nygren could end with the plea ". . . . not back to Luther, but forward to Luther. For he points the way to a deeper appreciation of the gospel of Christ. . . . When we issue the motto: 'Forward to Luther!' we would express the same thought in this way: Forward to the heart and center of the gospel, forward to the whole message of the gospel, forward to Christ who in the midst of death and human misery is the living and life-giving Word of God."[6]

It is an unfortunate historical accident, but one which cannot now be so easily undone, that we bear the name of Luther. Lutherans who boast of being Lutherans should, therefore, give heed to Luther's characteristically forceful words: "Who is this Luther? My teaching is not my own, and I have not been crucified for the sake of anyone . . . Why should it happen to me, miserable, stinking bag of worms that I am, that the children of Christ should be called by my insignificant name? . . . I am and will be nobody's master. With the one church I have in common the teaching of Christ who alone is our Master."[7]

So this is the first affirmation; that a peculiar *kairos* confronts the Lutheran Church at this moment, big with possibility in one direction or another, and it is not a presumption for the Lutheran Church to seek to speak a decisive word out of its heritage. It is a sincere act of self-surrender, with a prayer for the guidance of the Spirit, that the Word of God may really break through the earthen vessel.

[5] *The Proceedings of the Second World Assembly of the LWF, Hannover, Germany,* 1952, p. 53.
[6] *Ibid,* p. 49.
[7] *WA* 8, 685, 6.

LUTHERAN MOVEMENTS TOWARD UNITY

The peculiar *kairos* confronting the Lutheran Church must be seen now, first of all, on the background of its own movements toward unity. In the United States we have come a long way within this twentieth century from previous fragmentation (seventeen or more separate bodies) up to the present, which if present merger plans are completed will leave only three bodies: 1) the Synodical Conference (the Lutheran Church—Missouri Synod, the Joint Synod of Wisconsin, the Norwegian Synod, the Slovak Synod, the Negro churches), 2) the union of the American Lutheran Church, the Evangelical Lutheran Church, the United Evangelical Lutheran Church, the Lutheran Free Church, 3) the union of the United Lutheran Church, the Augustana Lutheran Church, the American Evangelical Lutheran Church, and the Suomi Synod, with the latter two further co-operating in the National Lutheran Council, and with friendly co-operation between all three groups, *e.g.* in student work, the Seminary Professors's Conference, and other informal study groups. For good or ill this marks a big step toward unity.

Secondly, there is the formation of the Lutheran World Federation which goes back to 1867—the meeting of the Lutheran General Conference—which slowly expanded from Germany to include Scandinavia and other countries. In 1911 there was a meeting at Uppsala with representation from the General Council of the United States. In 1917 the observance of the four hundredth anniversary of the Reformation, as well as the Catechism celebrations in 1929 and the Augsburg Confession in 1930, spurred efforts at unity. In 1923 there was held the first meeting of the International Inner Mission Association, as well as the first meeting of the Lutheran World Convention at Eisenach, at which the predominant figure was Archbishop Söderblom, the prodigious champion of ecumenicity on a sound, evangelical basis. His words of praise and warning deserve to be recalled at every gathering of Lutherans:

With profound gratitude in our hearts, we lift our voices in praise to God for His grace in sending the prophet, Martin Luther, to reveal to us again the atoning work of His Son. Scarcely a week of my life has passed since I was ordained, that I have not daily thanked God that I was born and brought up a Lutheran. For Luther is the greatest evangelist the Church of Christ has known since New Testament times. If most of us have that same feeling about Luther, it should not fill us with a sense of exaltation, but with a sense of serious responsibility. It should make us humble. For if we permit our Lutheranism to fill us with pharisaic self-satisfaction, then we need to remind ourselves of what Luther himself wrote in his first exposition of the Lord's Prayer: "Proud-spirited saints do more harm than any other people on earth." So then it is only *under* the name of Luther that we gather here. [8]

Then followed the second meeting of the Lutheran World Convention in 1929 with interest centering on Luther's Catechism, and a smaller meeting held in 1935. In 1936 Hanns Lilje became the first executive secretary of the Luthern World Convention. A meeting scheduled for Philadelphia in 1940 had to be canceled because of the war. After the war came the formation of the Lutheran World Federation with its first meeting at Lund in 1947, created as Dr. S. C. Michelfelder, its dynamic secretary, said, "to be a channel through which the gifts that God has given us may be shared and multiplied." In the statement of its sixfold purpose there is emphasis on the verbs: 1) to bear united witness before the world to the gospel of Jesus Christ as the power of God for salvation; 2) to cultivate unity of faith and confession among the Lutheran churches of the world; 3) to promote fellowship and co-operation in study among Lutherans; 4) to foster Lutheran participation in ecumenical movements; 5) to develop a united Lutheran approach to responsibilities in missions and education; 6) to support Lutheran groups in need of spiritual or material aid.

In 1952 there was Hannover and its theme, "The Living Word in a Responsible Church," with the church that had suffered under Nazi tyranny determined to get out of its ghetto and boldly proclaim God's Word as relevant to all of life.

[8] Quoted by E. Theodore Bachmann, *op. cit.*, p. 13.

THE ECUMENICAL MOVEMENT

Paralleling this movement toward world-wide Lutheran unity runs the ecumenical movement which should not be seen as in conflict with this growing confessional loyalty. The ecumenical movement goes back to the Evangelical Alliance meeting in London in 1846, the meeting of the World Conference on Missions in Edinburgh in 1910, and the meeting of the International Alliance for Friendship through the Churches in 1914. Then were formed the International Missionary Council, the International Sunday School Union (now the World Council on Christian Education), the World Student Christian Federation in which many of the present leaders of the ecumenical movement received their initial training, and the world YMCA and YWCA. The immediate forerunners of the World Council are, however, the twin Universal Christian Councils, the one on Life and Work (Stockholm, 1925; Oxford, 1937) turning to practical problems of ecumenical co-operation, and the other on Faith and Order (Lausanne, 1927; Edinburgh, 1937) with its attention directed toward theological bases.

Then came the formation of the World Council of Churches in Amsterdam in 1948, with the theme "Man's Disorder and God's Design," and the second meeting in Evanston in 1954, "Christ the Hope of the World."

Along with the formation of the World Council there has been the formation of international denominational groups, including Reformed, Anglican, Methodist, Congregational, Baptist, Presbyterian, and Disciples of Christ international alliances.

A GROWING CONFESSIONAL CONSCIOUSNESS

Accompanying the movement toward union of the denominations, there has been a growing confessional consciousness which is not to be viewed with alarm. Here the judgment of W.A. Visser 't Hooft is typical: "There are elements in the situtation that almost point in the direction of retrogression rather than in the direction of advance. There is no doubt that, since Amsterdam, certain confessional and denominational tendencies have become stronger than they were before. I find that some people are deeply worried about that. Personally, I do not consider that too dangerous or too tragic a development, because it is so inevitable. As soon as people are brought together in an ecumenical manner, they become more conscious of their own specific heritage. That happens internationally too. If an American wants to be made conscious that he is really American, let him go to Europe or to Asia.

"If a Lutheran or an Anglican or a Baptist wants to become conscious that he is that kind of Christian, let him attend an ecumenical conference. He will have to ask questions about his own denomination that he has never asked before. There is something of that in the whole picture of the ecumenical movement. But the question is this: Will that self-consciousness resulting from ecumenical contact be the end of the process? Or, will Christians work through that self-consciousness to a position where they say, 'Yes, we have a new understanding of our own heritage, but we also see that our heritage has its real meaning and sense and worth in the total fellowship of the ecumenical movement.' "

Noteworthy also are his words to the Third World Conference on Faith and Order: "Thirty years before when in Haelsingborg plans were made for the conferences of 'Life and Work' and 'Faith and Order' it was said: 'Service unites, but doctrine divides.' In the particular situation of those days the fear of a direct attack upon the fundamental differences between the churches can perhaps be understood. Today such a fear can only be considered as a pure anachronism. For we have had the opportunity to learn that so far from weakening our fellowship a frank and penetrating confrontation of our convictions is the only way to arrive at the

[9] W. A. Visser 't Hooft, *op. cit.,* p. 8.

deeper level of fellowship, the only level which is worthy of the Christian Church."[10]

Included in the picture should also be the fact that many churches of similar background and tradition have actually merged. Bishop Stephen Neill in *Towards Church Union, 1937-52,* records in that period thirteen achievements of complete organic union, two agreements for unconditional intercommunion, two for limited intercommunion, sixteen progressive negotiations with a view to organic union, seven with a goal of some kind of closer fellowship.

THE CHURCH OF SOUTH INDIA

Mention must also be made of the Church of South India, which in 1947 brought together the South Indian United Church, the South India Province of the Methodist Church, and the several dioceses of the Church of India, Burma, and Ceylon (Anglican), with the Baptists and Lutherans excluding themselves. This union is unique because for the first time it succeeded in bringing together churches both within and without the historic episcopal succession on the basis of agreement on the authority of the Scriptures, acceptance of the two ecumenical creeds, the two sacraments, and the historic episcopate on the following basis: "The Church of South India accepts and will maintain the historic episcopate in a constitutional form. But this acceptance does not commit it to any particular interpretation of episcopacy or to any particular view or belief concerning orders of the ministry, and it will not require the acceptance of any such particular interpretation or view as a necessary qualification for its ministry.

"Whatever differing interpretations there may be, however, the Church of South India agrees that, as episcopacy has been accepted in the church from early times, it may in this sense fitly be called historic, and that it is needed for the shepherding and extension of the church in South India. Any additional interpreta-

[10] Quoted by O. S. Tomkins, *The Third World Conference on Faith and Order, 1952* (London: Student Christian Movement. 1953), p. 129.

tions, though held by individuals, are not binding in the Church of South India."[11] A variety of doctrinal interpretations is thus allowed.

Doctrinal unanimity is not deemed inconsequential, but the urgency of uniting is considered to have priority, in the faith that living together will foster growing together in all essentials. In the so-called "Pledge" the uniting churches agree to respect each other's interpretations and ministries without prejudice.

This brief presentation can by no means do justice to what is involved. Anyone who delves into the vast literature *(see bibliography)* that has accumulated cannot but be impressed by this latest venture in ecumenicity but the question still arises whether or not the basis of union itself is not such that the Reformation might just as well not have occurred. Here the Anglicans have succeeded in maintaining their position adopted by the General Convention of the Episcopal Church in Chicago, in 1886, the Lambeth Conference in 1888, and restated in "An Appeal to All Christian People" issued by the Conference in 1920.[12]

To complete the picture a word should be said about the relation of Lutherans to the other evangelical churches of Germany. In Barmen (1934), Lutheran, Reformed, and United churches *(i.e.* containing both Lutheran and Reformed pastors and congregations, as for example in Prussia and Pomerania) united in a common confession (the Barmen Declaration), against a common foe but with no intention that this should dissolve their particular confessions.[13] After the war (1946) the Lutheran churches had

[11] *Constitution of the Church of South India* (Madras: Christian Literature Society for India, 1952), p. 9.

[12] See *The Christian Hope and the Task of the Church,* prepared by the Advisory Commission on the Main Theme, Evanston Assembly (New York: Harper, 1954), p. 25.

[13] *See the* Preamble *to the Barmen Declaration*: "Just because we wish to be and remain loyal to our various confessions, we may not be silent, since we believe that in this time of common need and trial a word common to us all is laid upon our lips. We commit to God whatever this may mean for the relation of the Confessional Churches among themselves." Quoted in *The Nature of the Church,* Ed. by R. N. Flew (New York: Harper, 1952).

to decide whether or not they would retain their confessional loyalty or sacrifice a certain *consensus in doctrine* for the sake of permanent union with the Reformed, with whom, under persecution, they had shared so much in common.

It soon became apparent that there were serious differences which followed along the historic lines on which the churches had divided originally (e.g. infant baptism, the Lord's Supper, the ministry, the relation between law and gospel, the doctrine of the two realms). So the Lutherans decided to stand together and in 1948 formed the United Evangelical Lutheran Church of Germany while at the same time, joining with the Reformed and United Churches to form the so-called Evangelical Church in Germany, a co-ordinating agency.

THE CONFESSIONAL STRUGGLE IN THE UNITED STATES

To return to the Lutheran Church in America, a review of the confessional struggles through which the Lutheran bodies passed shows one major concern consistently maintained, *viz.,* the concern for "purity of doctrine." Often, to be sure, there is revealed a proud assurance of being the sole possessors of the truth and often the concern for truth is caricatured into a fanatic insistence upon the intellectual acceptance of the whole of a man-made, time-bound system of doctrine. This does not alter the basic rightness of the position. Lutherans could not forget that when Luther reformed the church he didn't piddle around on the periphery, futilely fulminating with the incensed moralists of all times against the decadence of the times, but he went straight to the heart and center and blamed it all on false teaching, a basic misunderstanding of the gospel of the glory and the grace of God which alone is the true treasure of the church. Therefore his followers have always since insisted upon "the right proclamation of the gospel." Although it is idle to speculate, who knows what the history of the church in this country would have been like if it had not been for the Lutheran churches' loyalty to the confessions which obligated them to the gospel? Due to this loyalty they refused to open their pulpits to those whom they feared might mislead the people. If it is a matter of a common human quest for a solution to life's problems, then the pulpit may become a forum for all with a flare of genius to make their contribution, but not if it is a matter of faithful stewardship of the mysteries of God (I Corinthians 4:1) and the proclamation of a sure and certain word (II Peter 1:16). There is reason for the refusal to allow any and all to come to the altar to meet the living Lord of the church in either grace or judgment. If this is just an innocuous fellowship meal at which the devotees are reminded of the zeal of the Founder of their religion, what difference does it make who comes to share in the contagion of the charmed circle, but not so if "the Judge Eternal, to whom all nations bow, is with us now." [14]

The doctrinal declarations made from time to time concerned the following topics, beginning in 1868 with the discussion of the "four points," 1) chiliasm, 2) pulpit and 3) altar fellowship, 4) secret societies, which recur again, and then proceeding to "open questions," election (predestination and conversion), the church and the ministry, the attitude toward the confessions, the church and its external relationships, the Scripture as the Word of God. [15]

[14] See Luther's explanation of the first petition in both the Small and the Large Catechism. Also C. P. Krauth: *Theses on the Galesburg Declaration* (Philadelphia: The General Council, 1877).

[15] 1868—Pittsburgh Declaration, "4 points" (General Council)
1872—Akron, 1875, Galesburg Rule on pulpit and altar fellowship (General Council)
1873—The Davenport Theses, *Open Questions* (Missouri-Iowa).
1881—The Thirteen Propositions of the Missouri Synod Concerning Election (Prepared by C. F. W. Walther).
1908—The Toledo Theses, (1) The Church (2) The Office of the Ministry (3) Attitudes to the Confessions (4) Open Questions (5) Chiliasm (6) Predestination and Conversion (Iowa, 1908, Ohio, 1910).
1909—Richmond Resolutions, Statements Relative to the General Synod's Doctrinal Basis.
1912—Madison Agreement, On Election (Norwegian Lutheran Church)
1916—St. Paul Theses, On Election and Predestination (Missouri, Wisconsin, Iowa, Ohio).
1920—The Washington Declaration of Principles Concerning the Church and its External Relationship (ULCA).
1925—Minneapolis Theses, 1930 American Lutheran Conference: (1) The

Of these, it seems to me, the live issues are: the attitude toward the Scriptures (particularly the question of inspiration), the nature of confessional subscription, pulpit and altar fellowship (unionism), membership in secret societies (particularly on the part of the pastors). Something is said on these issues in a later chapter.

Mention should be made also of how consistently the Lutheran Church stood against the inroads of "modernism" which abandoned the decisive biblical witness and made of the Christian gospel merely the proclamation of certain universal truths and principles, the faith of Jesus, rather than faith in him. It is quite evident that Schleiermacher and Ritschl, who played such havoc with the gospel in Europe and also in American Protestantism in

Scriptures (2) The Lutheran Symbols (3) Church Fellowship (4) Points of Doctrine (The Work of Christ, the Gospel, Absolution, Holy Baptism, Justification, Faith, Conversion, Election) (5) The Lodge Question (Iowa, Ohio, Buffalo, Norwegian).

1925—The Intersynodical (Chicago) Theses, 1929, On Conversion and Election.

1932—Brief Doctrinal Statement of the Evangelical Lutheran Synod of Missouri, Ohio and other states, (1) Of the Holy Scriptures (2) Of God (3) Of Creation (4) Of Man and Sin (5) Of Redemption (6) Of Faith in Christ (7) Of Conversion (8) Of Justification (9) Of Good Works (10) Of the Means of Grace (11) Of the Church.

1934—The Savannah Resolutions, On Lutheran Unity (ULCA).

1938—The Baltimore Declaration, The Word of God (ULCA).

1940—The Pittsburgh Agreement, The Word of God (ULCA).

1949—The Common Confession

Part I—(1) God (2) Man (3) Redemption (4) Election (5) Means of Grace (6) Justification (7) Conversion (8) Sanctification (9) The Church (10) The Ministry (11) The Lutheran Confessions (12) The Last Things.

Part II—The Church in the World (i) The Church's Mission (ii) The Church's Resources (iii) The Church and its Ministrations (iv) The Church and the Home (v) The Church and Vocation (vi) The Church and Education (vii) The Church and Government (viii) The Church and Anti-Christian Organizations (ix) The Church and Anti-Christian Organizations (x) The Church and the World to Come (American Lutheran Church, Missouri Synod).

1925—United Testimony on Faith and Life.

Concerning Faith: I. God. II. Atonement. III. Means of Grace. IV. Justification. V. Sanctification. VI. The Church.

Concerning Life and Practice: I Liturgical Trends, II. Lay Activities in the Church, III. Elements in the Lord's Supper, IV. Christian Liberty, V. Concerning Evangelism, VI. Spiritual Fellowship (American Lutheran Conference)

1930—The Minneapolis Theses

general, made no inroads whatever on the officially taught Lutheran theology, because in all the synods without exception this remained the scholastic orthodoxy of the seventeenth century.[16] Unofficially, of course, there were many who were influenced by Schleiermacher, Ritschl, the social gospel, and many in their preaching and teaching departed from the biblical categories and preached a moral idealism more akin to Greek thought than to the biblical. The changed attitude toward the Bible, the advances of science, the findings of literary criticism which questioned the verbal inerrancy of all assertions in the Bible, and above all the inability to do justice to the gospel in the straitjacketing categories of Aristotelian scholasticism in which orthodoxy cast its theology after Luther had broken so decisively with these categories, left for many a theological vacuum into which drifted the strangest perversities.

Now that there has been a revival of orthodoxy in all of Protestantism on the basis of a dynamic conception of God's Word, and the Luther renaissance is literally opening up a whole new world, in which others than Lutherans are rejoicing, *the Lutheran Church stands in the most imminent danger of losing its heritage. It is at this point that American Lutheranism must listen to world Lutheranism as well as to the wider* oikumene *if its concern for "purity of doctrine" is not to betray it into drawing the battle line at the wrong place.*

PURITY OF DOCTRINE AND THE LWF

In the development of the Lutheran World Federation it is the same concern for the purity of the gospel which stands out es-

[16] See Schmid's *Doctrinal Theology of the Evangelical Lutheran Church,* Phila., 1876; H. E. Jacobs' *A Summary of the Christian Faith,* Phila., 1905; C. E. Lindberg's *Christian Dogmatics,* Rock Island, Ill., 1922; John T. Mueller's *Christian Dogmatics,* St. Louis, Mo., 1934; Franz A. O. Piper's *Christian Dogmatics*, 3 vols., St. Louis, Mo., 1950-53; Joseph Stump's *The Christian Faith,* Phila., 1942; Voigt's *Between God and Man,* Columbia, S. C., 1926; Milton Valentine's *Christian Theology,* Phila., 1906; R. F. Weidner's *Christology,* Chicago, 1913 (also treatments of other doctrines based on Luthardt); J. Michael Reu's unpublished mimeographed *Lutheran Dogmatics,* which shaped the theology of the Iowa Synod.

pecially in the part the federation played in the ecumenical movement. The fact that the ecumenical movement did not water down its doctrine to a lowest common denominator and that it was finally organized along confessional rather than geographical lines is due in great part to Lutheran influence. So Visser t' Hooft could say, in addressing the LWF at Hannover, that it is the Lutheran Church's historical task "to emphasize again and again that the main question in all discussions on the unity of the church is the quest for the pure gospel." In this way the ecumenical movement is helped "to resist the temptation of a superficial syncretism of creating unity by compromising. It is good and helpful for a sound development of the ecumenical movement that the Lutheran churches get together. For if churches of the same confession do not succeed in realizing the essential unity of the church, how should there be any hope for the wider *Oikumene?* In interdenominational contacts partners are required who know what they stand for and who are able to produce a common witness and common action."

If any still have misgivings about the World Council in any way intending to compromise the denominations, they should read the Toronto Statement adopted by the Central Committee in 1950, to which the Evangelical Lutheran Church of Hannover gave a typical reply: "The Lutheran Church possesses in the Confessio Augustana VII and VIII *(cf. also Apologia VII)* an expression of its conception of the Church. There is nothing in the ecclesiological statements by the World Council of Churches that would contradict these articles." [17]

The Lutheran World Federation is pledged by its constitution to participation in the ecumenical movement without compromise of its confessional position. This confessional position is, however, nothing but a pledge of loyalty to the Word of God rightly pro-

[17] *The Christian Hope and the Task of the Church* (New York: Harper, 1954), p. 16. See pp. 9 ff. for the Toronto Statement in abridged form.

claimed and it is this which will not be compromised. How this leaven of unwillingness to compromise the truth has permeated the leadership of the World Council can be amply documented. But at the same time there must be on the part of all genuine openness to the other, openness to the truth, openness to the enlightenment and guidance of the Holy Spirit. So says Visser 't Hooft: "For the sake of Christ's cause in the world it is no less necessary that intraconfessional co-operation will not be regarded as the final aim or as a means of defense against attempts visibly to express the unity of the whole Church of Christ."

Or this typical expression: "We all believe that the Church, which is the Body and the Bride of Christ, is something more than our own particular church tradition, and yet we all know that we can only *live* daily in the Body of Christ living faithfully in our own churches. The *status* of the World Council lies in accepting that paradox; its *dynamic* lies in refusing to accept it as final. The belief that enables the ecumenical movement to move lies in the unexplored territory of the sense in which the Body of Christ is more than our own Church and of the meaning of living faithfully within our Churches." [18]

While the World Council thus recognizes full denominational autonomy it is not to serve as an invitation to rest on our oars. "There are still many who think of the present relationship of our Churches in the World Council of Churches as an end rather than as a beginning, as a solution of the problem of unity rather than as a first step on the road to unity. The danger is that . . . the World Council can thus become a narcotic rather than a stimulant. We must react against this temptation of accepting the present established disorder of our ecclesiastical world simply because it has been made to look less shocking as it has been provided with an ecumenical varnish." [19]

[18] O. S. Tomkins, *op. cit.*, p. 163.
[19] *Ibid.*, p. 130.

THE BACKGROUND OF THE ASSEMBLY THEME

This is the larger background on which we approach our theme. Now for the more immediate one. The Hannover (Second Assembly of the LWF) theme was "The Living Word in a Responsible Church" and it was, in part at least, to make clear the fact that Lutheran attachment to the Word of God was not a dead-letter idolatry and to show the world that the church of the Reformation was at last, after the land of its birth had spawned the Nazi tyranny, crawling out of its ghetto and awakening to its social responsibility. Tremendous things had happened in the church and the world since World War I and at last it became apparent what a distortion of Luther's dynamic understanding of the gospel Lutheran quietism really is. So, like Luther, the church bearing his name once more spoke God's Word of judgment and grace boldly to the usurping tyrants as well as to those who were on the side of the children of light.

There is a play on words in the German which was partly lost in the translation. The responsible church must respond to the call and challenge of the living Word. To be responsible means to be under obligation to one who has a rightful claim upon you and to have to answer to him in word and in deed. It suggests also that, whatever the response, it is itself elicited by the challenge. It is the answer to an address; it does not arise from within; it is the response of one person as acted upon by another, not in mechanical I–It fashion but in the free decision of surrender. So the church cannot be the church and perform her tasks except as she is open to and responds in faith to her living Lord, present in Word and sacrament. Whatever was accomplished at Hannover, therefore, the intention at least was to rouse the church to her responsibility as she responds to the presence of the living Lord, who gives what he demands.

After Hannover it was the immediate wish of those looking ahead to the next assembly to proceed to a discussion of the church.

Instead, however, of beginning with a definition of the church such as, *e.g.,* in Article VII of the Augsburg Confession or an exposition of the creedal affirmation, "one, holy, catholic, apostolic church," it was agreed that the approach should be indirect. Therefore the third article (Of Sanctification) should be approached and understood from the point of view of the second, i.e. of Christology, the person and work of Christ in their totality. This should then not be divorced either from the doctrine of creation or the consummation of creation, remembering the dictum of the dogmaticians concerning the oneness of the acts of the Trinity, *opera ad extra indivisa sunt.* Then the church as the redeemed, restored, liberated, united people of God and the fulfilled creation will be seen in the totality of the one act of God in Christ.

The initial suggestion, therefore, was that we focus on what it means to be liberated by Christ, for this is what it means to be in the church. You cannot be liberated by Christ except by the incorporation into his body, which is the church, or vice versa into the church which is his body. Only by being a member of this body are you truly free, because you now find your proper place in the whole and are no longer enslaved by false freedom.

The original proposal was "Free Men in Christ" in order to point out what alone unites us and makes us one in the church, *viz.,* this fact that we have been liberated by Christ. This would really speak from the heart of the Reformation and shout out the glad cry to a people enslaved, it would seem, as never before, inside the church by a disastrous confusion of law and gospel[20] and outside the church by the demonic phenomenon of the enslaved mass man, just at the time when the vast progress in learning and education and all the vaunted advances of science should be liberating them. So the central doctrine of Lutheranism, the doctrine of justification by grace alone for Christ's sake through faith unto good works, sometimes so disastrously foreshortened,

[20] See, *e.g.* Canon Theo. Wedel: *The Christianity of Main Street* (New York: Macmillan, 1950).

could be developed in its full dimensions, and the heart of God laid bare. It is said with sufficient justification that the problem of most people today in our Western society is not, as it was for Luther in his day, how to find a gracious God as opposed to the angry God of medieval piety, but how to find meaning and purpose in life in the face of events which conspire in a thousand ways to empty life of all meaning and purpose. The problem today, it is said, is that modern man is unable to believe in any God whatever. But to pit the search for the gracious God against the search for meaning and purpose in life is nonsense. Communists and idealists of all kinds find meaning and purpose enough in life, and even nihilists and atheistic existentialists succeed in facing life in bold defiance of its ultimate end in nothingness. Human nature has the most marvelous capacity for self-deception and "Stoic" (in the popular sense) resolution. So the real problem is always how to be found of the gracious God in order to escape the judgment under which one always is apart from thus being apprehended. The problem is not whether there be *a* "god," for this word in itself is only a scribble on a page or a breath of more or less foul air, depending on the state of a man's halitosis *(flatus vocis),* or a convulsion of the larynx, until it be defined. The problem is always as to the nature and inner disposition of that "unknown Other" (in the sense of "the holy") of whose presence all men are inescapably aware, even though they ignore or defy him. The real problem at all times, in the midst of the insecurity, guilt, anxiety, tragedy, meaninglessness of existence, even in its moments of bliss and highest exaltation, is whether or not there is a God who cares and is capable of doing anything about it. The speculations of the philosophers are rife enough with hypotheses concerning a good God too weak to help or a strong God too preoccupied to care. The question is whether there is a God who is both willing and able to help and what he has done about it. So this takes us right back to the heart and center of the gospel and that central article by which the church will stand or fall.

The theme "Free Men in Christ" was proposed as reiterating the heart of the gospel, but because there were some who thought that there should be a more explicit emphasis upon unity, the combination of being both freed and united by Christ was suggested. This struck fire, and it was agreed that the combination of freedom and unity follows naturally and inescapably. It is impossible to be freed by Christ without being united with God, with the neighbor, with oneself. To be freed by Christ is to be united by Christ; if we are one in Christ it is only because we are freed by him and vice versa. This must take place, this must happen. Men have *to be freed* and *be united* in Christ and this can happen only where the gospel is rightly proclaimed and the sacraments administered in harmony with that proclamation.

The original wording "Freed and United by Christ Alone," was then changed to the present tense, "Christ Frees and Unites," because while the former correctly emphasizes that once-and-for-all act of liberation and unification which is the beginning of the new age and the Christian church, it does not put the emphasis where it really belongs, on the *now,* that moment which is for each the fulness of time, in which the Christ frees and unites again and again, and that, therefore, it is not in the final analysis a matter of defining the church as something static but of being the church in each succeeding moment of repentance and faith.

So the doctrine of the church must have at its very heart and center the liberating, uniting act of God in Christ. When Luther reformed the church he did not seek to patch around here and there on a garment that needed replacing altogether. He went to the center and like the matchless "systematic theologian" that he was he built up, with the utmost consistency and with deliberate disregard of the contradictions in which he became involved, a qualitatively different whole, true to the biblical witness. It is only if, like him, we work out from this center that we can come to a solution of our problems, first of all in achieving Lutheran unity, and then, also, in speaking to the wider unity of the church.

It is exactly to this same conclusion that "Faith and Order" came in Lund in 1952. Interfaith discussions had reached an impasse, a crisis in the method of procedure. For years the churches had been making the most painstaking comparisons and trying to reach a maximum of agreement. They had studied both "the agreements within the disagreements and the disagreements within the agreements" as Edmund Schlink suggested.[21] But this statistical method which, as Schlink says, presupposes "a certain static structure in the churches which are to be compared with one another," has reached its limits; it doesn't reckon with changes and it demands no sacrifices. This crisis in method is accompanied by the crisis caused by the persecution of the churches calling for a united opposition; furthermore also by the progress toward unity made by some of the younger churches, and finally by the actual experience of unity which innumerable people in ecumenical contacts have felt. We cannot, therefore, just continue talking about unity, but talk must issue in action.

This then is the way that we must walk together, back to the center in Christ. "The way to the center is the way to unity" (Nygren). It is here that the *kairos* presents itself to the Lutheran Church. This has been her persistent cry, to go to the center, to the gospel, to Christ himself.[22] On this basis Lutherans ought first of all to demonstrate their unity to the world. Whether or not they are all united in one organization will be for the moment a secondary matter, for if only there is agreement on what the gospel really is, then the rest will follow. This is the thrust of the theme "Christ Frees and Unites." It is the living Christ who himself frees and unites us. Nothing matters except this gospel of the liberating and uniting Christ, but this matters supremely and this determines everything else that matters.

[21] Edmund Schlink, "The Pilgrim People of God" in O. S. Tomkins, *op. cit.*, p. 156.
[22] See Anders Nygren, *Christ and His Church* (Philadelphia: Westminster, 1956).

II

The Freedom and Unity Given to Us in the Church

Freedom and unity! These are precisely the two possessions which man, the thinking reed (Pascal), has presumed from time immemorial. This is the claim the Greeks, whose heirs we all are, made for man's immortal soul. In spite of the bondage of the body and its disintegration, the soul that dwells within this passing house is free and one, without beginning or end, self-dependent and self-sufficient, indestructible, an integer without parts, and therefore unable to disintegrate. Man, the rational being, the man of integrity! Freedom and unity are his inherent possessions; they belong to his very being and make him what he is.

Or, if freedom and unity are not inherent qualities, then they are something which man can achieve for himself. In various forms this endeavor recurs until it takes the form of the rich fool of the twentieth century who multiplies his possessions, his gadgets, his libraries, his *objets d'art,* his wives, his children, his fornications, and his religions in order to raise himself to that coveted place of unhampered wholeness and harmony.

MAN'S ACTUAL SITUATION

Against these proud claims and frantic endeavors stands the witness of the centuries, the tragedy of life itself, that makes man its pawn and tears him into shreds. There stands the actual man, the man of history who is born of woman's pain, lives in anxiety and fear, hungers and is satisfied, hates and loves, aspires, falls, picks himself up only to fall again until finally he fails to rise. This includes the philosopher himself who does not live in the magnificent castle of his thought, but in a miserable hovel by its side (Kierkegaard). This man is not in possession of freedom and unity; neither can he achieve it. He is actually enslaved and estranged. He is the man in contradiction to his origin, to himself, and to his brother. So, according to the witness of the Bible, there stands at the very beginning of human history an act of enslavement and estrangement. Man is driven out of paradise, he no longer beholds the face of God, both he and the world over which he is set to rule are under a curse. He goes out a stranger and a pilgrim with the hand of his own flesh and blood turned against him, and of the first pair of brothers the one is a murderer.

MAN CONSTITUTED BY HIS RELATIONS

This takes us into that other, strange, and different world of the Bible where freedom and unity are not a present possession or, for that matter, qualities at all which could inhere in man and make him what he is. This is, perhaps, something the modern man can readily understand, because the so-called uncuttable 'atom' has ceased to be. The atom has been split and the storehouse of energy within it has been released, making it clear that the whole physical world is a matter of relations. In it nothing is stable and things are what they are because of their relations, and when the delicate balance is disturbed there is an explosion to rock and roll the world. From seething cauldron to refreshing fountain, from morning mist to impenetrable murk, it is a matter of relations. And the same is true of man. He is not a free and unified, self-contained atom, but a center of relations who must be made unified and stable and must be given his equilibrium, who is in constant jeopardy and is freed and united only so long as the relationships in which he is keep him as such. But here we must anticipate and we must warn against reducing man to nothingness, as the Communists and atheistic existentialists do when they dissolve man completely into his relations, like peeling an onion, until you have nothing left but the tears. There is that center of responsibility, that person with a name whom God has brought forth out of nothingness and whom God sustains throughout all the physical changes. He cannot escape God by dying, but passes through death to the resurrection and is inextricably tied up with hands and feet and eyes and heart and stomach with father and mother and brother and bread and wine and the lion and the lamb, with all of which he will one day share the glorious liberty of the children of God.

The only one who does not depend for his being free and one upon relations is the God who is the ground and origin and sustainer of all relations. And even of him himself we cannot assert that he has freedom and unity because his freedom he has chosen to limit and in his oneness he is triune. This is the difference between the God of the Bible and other, man-made gods. The God of the Bible is the living God. He is not love in a static sense of definition, but is the God who loves and who lays bare his inmost disposition to man when he comes to him, enters into the most intimate relationship with him, chooses himself a bride and knows only her in unwavering, steadfast love and fidelity. The verbs in the Bible are the important words and not the nouns. The God of the Bible is the God who acts. He is not the ideal that sits serenely in the sky and shines for man's spectator contemplation. God is not beauty in the Bible, but he is the God who adorns the world with beauty, paints the sunsets and the autumn leaves, clothes the lilies of the field with glory and puts the pallor and the brightness on the beloved's cheek. He is not truth, but he is the one who, as man faces the impenetrable portals, takes him by the hand and leads him through the opened door. He is not goodness, but he is the one who comes to the sinner and eats with him, and covers him and changes him with his own righteousness.

He is not wrath, but he is the one who takes whip in hand and consumed with holy zeal for his house drives the moneychangers from the temple and consigns the hypocrites to the outer darkness where there is nought but weeping and gnashing of teeth. It is he who is able to destroy both body and soul in hell who alone is to be feared.

This is—if the word itself will not frighten the suspicious—the biblical-existential background on which we must view that act of God in Christ whereby man is freed and is united. Men are freed and united by God's own act of self-impartation and with this we have the heart of the gospel as the Reformation gave it back to the world; the Copernican revolution which really makes God and not man the center with everything dependent upon him. Here is the true Jacob's ladder whereon God climbed down to man to meet him on his anxious flight from himself and his brother and to reintegrate and reunite him. This is the end of the toilsome climb up the ladder to the beatific vision which is still the way of Roman Catholicism today with the church conveniently supplying the necessary infusions of sanctifying and actual grace. Here the flow of love is altogether down and out and never in an I–It way of infusions of power through inert media, but always in the personal encounter with the living God, present to all men in the "masks" of creation and present in the fulness of his love in Word and sacrament in the living body of the church of which the incarnate, risen, ascended, present Christ is the living Head.

Furthermore, it must be said at the outset that the "and" which connects the act of freeing and the act of uniting is not additive. There are not two acts which follow one after the other, but they are inseparably one. They can be distinguished *(unterschieden)* but not separated *(geschieden-getrennt)*. In one sense the act of liberation has a certain priority and is basic, but in another sense this is true also of the act of unification. Actually they are like the sailor who "sailed before the mast"—mast and sailor set out on the great adventure together.

AN ACT OF ENSLAVEMENT AND ESTRANGEMENT

In the third place, as already indicated, the act of liberation presupposes a definite act of enslavement and estrangement, disintegration and dispersion. It is not possible to equate man's predicament in existence either with his finitude (the fact that his soul is imprisoned in the body, or that his fingers are not firm enough so that his reach exceeds his grasp, or that he still carries too much of the freightage of his animal ancestry) or with a blind, inscrutable relentless fate *(moira)*, as meaningless as it is arbitrary (cf. the Greek tragedies in which the tragedy lies in the fatal clash of two genuinely heroic figures, both of whom succumb). There is rather a deliberate act of enslavement and estrangement which is God's act of judgment upon guilt. This is the significance of the biblical story of the fall which, like the biblical witness throughout, does not mean to convey a universal, everywhere discernible truth of the reason. It witnesses to a historical event which actually happened at a time and place but its meaning is discernible only to faith and not to a disinterested spectator who eavesdrops as the serpent talks to Eve and Eve in turn seduces Adam with an apple. So the Bible witnesses unequivocally to an actual historical fall standing at the beginning of human history. We know no history apart from this, for on the level of that which involves no freedom and no decision, there is by definition no history and, therefore, history begins with God's act of creation in love as well as with the fall and with God's judgment upon it.

THE MYSTERY OF THE EVIL ONE

Finally there is one more presupposition—from my experience perhaps the most difficult to get across in its devastating profundity—"the mystery of the Evil One," that will in the world which would not let us hallow God's name nor let his kingdom come, that enslaving will into whose awful power we have been committed, because we are, all together—for in isolation no one exists—a fallen race. It is that disrupting, scattering, dividing will that sets man against God in proud mistrust and rebellion, man against himself in frightful disintegration, and brother against brother in anger, jealousy, hatred, until he destroys the very thing he loves. Without trying to explain the cause of evil in the world or trying to extricate man from his full responsibility and guilt, this will antedates and is separate from the will of man or the wills of all men put together, while nevertheless he is not a co-god but himself the creature of God. This is Satan, the Adversary, "who goeth about as a roaring lion seeking whom he may devour." Without this dramatic struggle between God and Satan the whole act of liberation and unification would most certainly have to be described differently than it is in the biblical witness. Moreover, there is again a reflection of man's pride in his determination to take all the credit for evil to himself, rather than to admit its unsolved mystery. The evil in the world is too awful; man can't be that much of a devil.

Without these presuppositions, then, of the event of creation out of love (so that God is not the creator of evil), of a historical fall (for which the creature himself is responsible), of the existence of Satan, God's Adversary, and of a judgment (which is God's judgment upon the guilty), the act of liberation cannot be understood as an act in history which is God's decisive act of lifting the judgment and the curse and beginning a renewed creation and a new aeon. God is the actor all the way through and throughout he is the one who acts in love. In love he creates, in love he pronounces the judgment upon the guilty, for it is only love which has been offended. In love he comes to redeem, to lift the judgment, to cover the sin, to lift the curse, to free from bondage, to recreate, to restore, to reunite, to reintegrate, to make whole the fragmented by making right the relationships upon which the very being of the dependent, responsible creature depends. Only as the creature responds in receptivity and trust to the word of love addressed to him is he the true *humanus,* properly reflecting that image of God which is love. Man is like the moon which has no light of its own, but shines only as it reflects the borrowed light of the sun and this depends on its rotations and the degree to which it turns with open face to reflect the full-orbed glory of that light in which there is no variableness or shadow produced by turning (James 1:17). The orientation must be right and all obstructions removed.

Just so it is with man, who, turned in upon himself and the world (Luther's *incurvatus in se*) and unable to reflect that true light which was in the world from the beginning, and then came into his own in the world at a point in space and time, must be straightened out, that he may reflect that love in, for, and by which he was made.

MAN'S BONDAGE AND DISPERSION

On the basis of these presuppositions we can then briefly sum up the bondage and the dispersion in which man is. Enough has been said in our day in description and diagnosis of the enslavement of modern man; so much so that it is about time to call a halt and to say something constructive on the other side, as we shall do in good time in emphasizing the civil righteousness of which man is capable. There is the emphasis upon his insecurity, his loss of personal worth, his loneliness and lack of fellowship, due to the breakdown of erstwhile inviolable authorities, of former patterns of community and the increasing mechanization, rationalization, and urbanization of life which produced the mass man. In a sense, the basic problem of modern man is his loss of freedom and unity, aggravated by the fact that all the advances of science, which have given man such unprecedented control over his environment and which have brought the whole world into a neighborhood, have not been able really to free and unite men, but have constituted a Frankenstein conjured up to enslave and disunite. This is particularly true when we remember that there are much more subtle means of coercion and enslavement than the obvious use of force and the power of the sword. Man is coerced and robbed of the freedom of responsible decision by modern mass methods of communication, by clever psychological techniques which culminate in brainwashing by means of the injection of drugs, so that he is no longer inner-self-directed but outer-other-directed.[1] In the midst of plenty he is in dire want, surrounded by safeguards he is insecure, precisely as the object (*i.e.* the thing) of such excessive solicitude he becomes "nobody" and is ruthlessly experimented upon and brutally pushed around. This is reflected *ad nauseam* in modern literature, drama, art with their recurrent theme of meaninglessness and frustration, in the fantastic return to religion, and in the lucrative popularity of peace-of-mind cults.

But this is not the whole story. Sometimes one gets the impression from "Christian" fulminations against the worldliness of the world that apart from the specific gospel of Christ man is always the *homo lupus,* the rapacious wolf of Hobbes' "war of all against all." The reformers, however, recognized that even the fallen man is still capable of a "civil righteousness," in virtue of what was called the "remnant of the image of God." Luther particularly recognized this—quite contrary to the common estimate according to which Luther's doctrine of the bondage of the will and of total depravity would make man altogether incapable of any kind of goodness. The Formula of Concord explicitly refutes the notion that man's *essence* after the fall is sin.[2] Luther simply opposed the quantitative view of the Roman Church, according to which man's natural and rational faculties remain unimpaired after the fall so that for him to achieve the supernatural virtues in addition to the natural ones, only a supplementation of powers through successive infusions of grace is necessary. He held instead that man, in his totality, is affected by the wrong relationship in which he is by nature (cf. the *sine vera metu, sine vera fiducia, et cum con-*

[1] See David Riesman, *The Lonely Crowd* (New Haven: Yale University Press, 1950); also *Changing America,* mimeographed study document of the World Council of Churches.

[2] See H. E. Jacobs, *The Confessions* (Philadelphia: United Lutheran Publication House, 1893), pp. 539ff.

cupiscentia of Art. II of the Augsburg Confession). This made it conclusively impossible for him to achieve a "goodness" or "righteousness" in the strength of which he could stand in the judgment. He is always a sinner, because he is in the wrong God-relationship, and until this relationship is straightened out, he can do nothing really God-pleasing; he cannot really reflect the pure *agape* in, for, and by which he was made and become the clear channel for this love to flow in and through him to the neighbor and the world's needs. He cannot, therefore, become good by doing good. He must first be good, before he can do good, in a straightened-out relationship.

But this would not keep him from being a "good man" as men reckon "goodness." It was for this reason that Luther was willing to turn the government and the ordinary affairs of life over to man, provided only he would use the brains and other powers God had given him and discern the law written in his heart (Romans 2:14). Man could in this way achieve a measure of life-together and could do so-called good works without thereby achieving a righteousness before God in the place of justification *(coram deo, in loco justificationis).* Whatever actual righteousness he possesses will be the result of the fact that no man can ever be outside of the God-relation. Virtues, in this view, are not qualities inhering in an essence. They are modes of behavior in a relationship and the God of *agape* is inescapably related to man in the "masks" of creation. Out of this relation there grow the so-called *splendida vitia* (splendid vices) of the heathen and all those humanitarian concerns for which men in their pride are wont to take credit. They are good for what they are good for, and should be recognized as such, but they are not good enough to redeem the sinner or to free him for his basic bondage and disintegration.

So in spite of the area of freedom in which man moves and the measure of integrity and oneness he is able to achieve there is a basic bondage "from which he can in no wise set himself free" and an estrangement from God, from his "true self" and from the brother from which no man can extricate himself any more than he can point to the end of his finger with the point of that same finger. This is the human situation, *i.e.* the situation of man in his existence before God, perennially the same, now as when Adam lost his paradise, when Jews clamored for a sign and crucified the Lord of glory, and when Greeks sought for wisdom and heaped scorn upon the foolishness of the cross and resurrection, when today the multitudes wander like sheep without a shepherd.

This bondage and this estrangement result from the fact that man, under the conditions of his finitude and his freedom the concomitant anxiety does not take his life from God in trust and does not become the clear channel for God's love to flow through him to the neighbor.[3] As the result of this wilfully disturbed God-relationship he is in the bondage of the tyrants we have already intimated. He is under both the guilt and the power of sin. He is a sinner at all times and does not just on occasion commit this or that sin. He is therefore under God's judgment and the wrath of God and it is God himself who gives him over to the consequences of his sin and the tyrants who hold him in thrall (Romans 1:18ff). If it is God who does this, then only God is strong enough to cope with God; and, since God is love, it is only love which can cope with wrath and enable man to stand in the judgment.

Furthermore, man is now under the dominion of the devil, because in his sinning he is delivered over to this alien power, which possesses him (heteronomy) (Romans 7:14, "The evil that I would not, that I do") just as he is in his God-given righteousness filled with and possessed by the Spirit of Christ in, for, and by which he was made (theonomy) ("I live, nevertheless not I, but Christ lives in me," Galatians. 2:20). The devil in him is never the cause of his sinning, because cause and effect are the wrong categories, but when a man sins it is the devil who has his way with him.[4] It is the whole field of relationship (the demonic

[3] See Lutheran World Supplement, "Christ Frees and Unites," Geneva, 1956.
[4] See C. S. Lewis, *The Screwtape Letters* (New York: Macmillan, 1943).

structures) which is wrong and this is the bondage and the disintegration.

There is also the bondage of the law. An act of love must be freely and spontaneously done, welling up from within for the sake of the beloved and not squeezed and scourged out by pressures and flayings. But the law is a cruel taskmaster and man is unable to achieve the freedom of love, because this is a contradiction—thou shalt love! This is the sign of our bondage! Since we must be commanded to love, it is certain that we are not free! Moreover, love must always be free and flexible to do what the moment demands, while he who is under the law is in a straitjacket that makes impossible the unexpected, unpredictable, extravagant act of love, poured out in profusion, sending out its fragrance to the dismay of the starched scribes and hectic humanitarians of all times.

Finally, there is the bondage of death and that final disruption which eventually tears all loved ones apart—the real disintegration of death, the foulness and the corruption and the nothingness of it—which to the one who is offended is "such a dirty trick" (Ernest Hemingway), and to the believer is "the wages of sin." Because the God-relation is not right, there is this last and final enemy. Before this power man does indeed stand absolutely helpless and it is this that God means to teach man by his dying. Because all are sinners all must die. This, indeed, is a realization that comes only after the right God-relation has already been established. For it does not result from the review of the mortality statistics, nor from that awful "ontological shock" (Paul Tillich) when man is shot to the quick with the realization that he could also not be, and that he does not have within himself the power to resist the flow of blood once the artery has been cut or to give himself air when the heart is no longer pumping and he is choking to death. The realization that the wages of sin is death results only from the confrontation with the living God in both judgment and grace.

Man's inner disharmony, the world-wide phenomenon of the

guilty conscience, the sinister awareness that all is not well within constitute a bondage which in the very nature of the case man cannot take away from himself. It is the result of the disturbed relation which must be set right from the side of the one in whom the relation has its *fons et origo.* Every effort to achieve freedom is by its very nature only a flailing around within the prison walls, only a railing of the justly accused against his accuser. The loneliness and the "shut-upness" that estranges a man from his neighbor, whose acceptance he fears if that neighbor really got a look into his heart, is a doorless, windowless prison. The very nature of life-together in which each serves the other with his gifts in free spontaneity for his sake while at the same time so finding self-fulfilment is destroyed by the incurable egocentricity (Luther's *incurvatus in se*). Man is chained by his past and is not open to his future. Behind him lies the irrevocable past, before him the unpredictable future, and both shout their accusations and their fears in the moment, while in a thousand frantic ways man tries to cover that past and build his bulwarks against the future.

THE GOOD NEWS OF THE LIBERATOR

Now it is the gospel, *the good news,* that at a time and place in history, in the fulness of time, in the decisive, crucial *kairos* which marks the turning point of all history, after a period of preparation, there took place in the act of God in Christ the once and for all decisive liberation and unification. This was "God in Christ reconciling the world unto himself." No lesser being, not one like unto the Father, but only he who was of one essence with the Father, only the very love of very God himself entered into human flesh could achieve this liberation and unification.

There is no time to spell out in detail this "objective," decisive act of reconciliation and redemption, but it means a change of relationship from wrath to peace (Ephesians 2:14ff.), reconciliation, and a liberation from the powers that held men in thrall, *i.e.,* redemption. Since we have gone to such trouble to describe the chains, it should be easy to see that here now is the loosening of the chains that man could not loosen for himself and, therefore, the beginning of a new age for all mankind, in which the decisive victory has already been won although the battle continues.

This is the real *Christus Victor* theme which pervades Luther's explanation of the Second Article, but which has sometimes become falsely subordinated to the penal and forensic aspects of the atonement. This aspect dare not be neglected (if one really listens to the biblical witness!), but it must be incorporated with the dominant motif, to join in the harmony of the glad song of liberation and unification. This is liberation in the sense in which it frees from the bondage we have described. And together with it and inseparable from it is the unification in the sense of the end of the estrangement, the disharmony, and the disintegration we have described! There is the life-creating righteousness of God in Christ which both covers the sin and recreates to newness of life. It must be so understood that it may all be summed up in the forgiveness of sins and we can say with Luther, "Therefore the true and only religion, the only true divine worship, is to believe in the free forgiveness of our sins, without works, out of pure grace alone. . . . To trust in this God who is gracious to us out of pure love and who does us good 'for nothing,' that is the true religion and the true righteousness." [5]

In this view, therefore, Jesus is not the founder of a new religion whose teachings men are to follow, but he himself in his person is the Liberator and the Uniter. In his person in the mystery of the incarnation, the divine and the human were once and for all united. It is this divine-human Lord who suffers and dies and is resurrected and exalted on high to send the Spirit and the Head of the church.

Of course, the claim is not made that this is the only and final way in which these matters can be formulated. The meaning of the gospel always has to be spelled out anew in each new situa-

[5] *WA* 26, 287.

tion in refutation of false alternatives, but, for our purpose in this specific context, since we are trying to determine what the church is from the central act of God in Christ, the meaning should be clear enough. It is, we said, a matter of right relations and this involves man not only in his God-relation, but also in his relation to himself and to his brother, as well as to all creation. To interpret Christian freedom as individualism and isolation from the brother, as some kind of autonomy, is the grossest kind of misunderstanding. There is no Christian apart from Christ, and there is no Christ apart from the brother who mediates that Christ to him. Liberated brother is therefore equally bound to liberated brother in love in the universal priesthood. This means the Christian *koinonia* as the fellowship of the liberated and united.

THE LIBERATED AND UNITED PEOPLE OF GOD

This is what Israel was from the beginning, a covenant people, chosen from among the nations of the world in love, and betrothed to him as a bride even though, like Hosea's harlot wife, they had already been unfaithful, and then repeatedly had to be bought back again after repeated acts of unfaithfulness, until there came that final and decisive act of redemption (literally "buying back"), the price of which was the suffering of God himself. The twelve tribes of Israel are therefore replaced by the twelve apostles as the beginning of the new Israel. Circumcision is replaced by baptism as God's act of acceptance into the new covenant relation based on Calvary and in it the believer is baptized into Christ's death and rises to a new life of fellowship with Father, Son, and Holy Ghost in the church. This church is the *koinonia,* the congregation of believers *(congregatio sanctorum)* who are joined to Christ in faith and in him to each other. He is the vine, they are the branches; he is the head, they the body (*corpus Christi*); he is the bridegroom, they the bride; he is the cornerstone, they the building with the apostles the foundation. They are the *coetus electorum,* called out of darkness into marvelous light; they are the first fruits of the harvest and the new creation.

The vexing question as to which comes first, the individual or the church, or whether there is any salvation outside of the church, is simply settled if the whole matter is seen as being in relationship to Christ as one member of his body inseparable from the other members. The God-relation is, as always, a mediated relationship so that the individual members of Christ's body are joined to him only through the brother and the brothers to each other only in Christ. No one today would know of Christ except through the witness of the brother who brings him Christ, thus becoming a Christ to him. Christ did not—like the other founders of religion—leave behind him a dictated body of teachings. He chose twelve apostles, a select body of witnesses, and he not only left behind him a witnessing community, but he himself remained present in that witnessing community. Nowhere is the dependence of brother upon brother clearer than here. *Agape* service consists of serving the brother with the gifts you possess and the brother lacks. The brother who has the gospel and with it the living Christ will therefore be under the constant constraint of love to bring that gospel to the neighbor. And what he brings him is not a truth but Christ himself as liberator and unifier.

The church is thus both the creation and the workshop of the Holy Spirit. This means that on the first Pentecost, when the Holy Spirit came upon the disciples, the church came into being as the body of believers and these believers in turn became the witnesses to bring others into the church in the same way that they themselves had come in, when in the proclamation of the good news of the crucified and risen Christ, God in Christ had come to them and they were baptized into his death and raised with his resurrection to newness of life (Romans 6:4). The believer is brought into being by a witness and he himself in turn becomes a witness, so where there is the witness, the gospel proclaimed, there are sure to be believers, and where there are belivers there is in turn the witness. So the living Christ is mediated by the brother in the "mediated immediacy" of the real presence of God which is no less immediate and no less mediated than the presence of God in the "masks" of creation or anywhere else where the unseen and unseeable God personally encounters man.

This oneness of the body of Christ and the believers is then also realized in the only other rite practiced among the believers ostensibly at the Lord's command from the very beginning, *viz.* the Lord's Supper. All that we have said is not only symbolized but actualized here. This meal is the abrogration as well as the fulfilment of the Passover meal. The pilgrim people look back upon that decisive act of deliverance upon Calvary, celebrate the presence of the risen and victorious Christ, and feed upon the body given and the blood shed for them, and look forward to the final, full, face-to-face fellowship in the new heaven and the new earth.

THE ONENESS OF THE CHURCH

That the church of Christ is actually one, that it is an actual, visible fellowship of flesh-and-blood men and women should now be quite clear. This oneness is a gift; it exists; it is not something still to be achieved; it exists as an actual relationship and contemporaneity with the same incarnate, risen, living Christ. Thus Christ and his church are one, and nothing, no party factions as in Corinth, or false teaching as in Galatia, can destroy this essential oneness.

Since the relation to the person of the historical Jesus is thus the decisive thing, since it was he who called all men unto himself, and promised, after he was lifted up, to draw all men unto himself, then this resurrected and risen Lord must actually continue to be present among men through the years, to invite, to console, to judge, to atone, to forgive, and to effect all that liberation and unification of which he has spoken. *He is thus present to men wherever the gospel is rightly proclaimed and the two sacraments administered according to that gospel.* How else and where else is he to be present? This accounts for Luther's emphasis upon the Word, the *viva vox evangelii,* for only in the Word is he present as the gracious God who imparts himself. This presence, whether it be in the Word of forgiveness or in the Word of the sacraments, is always the real presence of him who became incarnate, was obedient unto death, and therefore was highly exalted. (Philippians 2:5ff.). If this is not the same Christ and if in this Christ there is not the same God who made the worlds, then the whole conception of the church breaks down. Quite obviously this Christ can be present only where the gospel of his act of liberation and unification is rightly proclaimed. "Ye shall be my witnesses from Jerusalem throughout Judea and Samaria to the uttermost parts of the earth." So the living Christ is carried, not indeed in a monstrance but in the Word of proclamation embodied in living witnesses, from land to land and year to year, in endless unbroken succession—the *viva vox evangelii,* coming to life in the power of the Holy Spirit and so captivating and empowering to belief the lost of every nation, kindred, and tribe, calling them out of the kingdom of darkness into marvelous light.

In their lifetime the disciples had been united in a *koinonia* of love by the Christ who not only accepted them in their sin but suffered innocently for their sin, and he had, therefore, given them his own sacrificed body and blood, that they might live by it. He had said that he would not drink of the fruit of the vine until he drank it with them again in the perfected kingdom of heaven. So they looked forward to that joyful reunion with him at the heavenly banquet table. But in the meantime he was veritably in their midst, reassuring them of his gracious presence wherever the gospel was proclaimed and the sacraments administered. What else are we to conclude than that the one, holy, catholic, apostolic church consists of all who are liberated and united by that Christ who is present in the gospel rightly proclaimed and the sacraments administered in harmony with that gospel?

III

Christian Freedom and the Unity of the Church

The previous chapter tried to describe the liberating and uniting act of God in Christ which creates the one people of God, freed and united in this Christ as his body the church.

There is thus no question about the oneness of the church. More than one is simply a contradiction and yet this contradiction exists in the actual churches. Every Christian must be inwardly torn by this state of affairs. On the one hand he feels impelled to give full outward expression to the already existing unity. On the other hand he is unwilling to have this outward unity "at any price"; the outward unity must be in harmony with the unity that Christ actually establishes. It must be unity in the truth (John 17:17-21; I Timothy 3:15; Acts 2:42). The boundaries of the church must be clearly defined. The church must be no more exclusive and no more inclusive than her very nature demands; no larger and no smaller than the actually given dimensions.[1]

THE DISTINCTION BETWEEN "VISIBLE" AND "INVISIBLE" CHURCH

At this point the distinction between the visible and invisible church is neither help nor consolation. Such a distinction, if it is not further clarified, plays directly into the hands of making the

[1] See also R. L. P. Hanson, *Summons to Unity* (London: Edinburgh House Press, 1954), p. 15.

church into a Platonic ideal,[2] a so-called inner, spiritual relationship of souls incapable, because of the conditions of finitude, of finding actual embodiment in a real fellowship of flesh-and-blood men and women who share not only the same thoughts but are joined in an intimate fellowship of body, life, possessions. A successful repudiation of this view depends upon the realization of the oneness of the person in body and soul as entering in his totality into the right God-relationship in Christ through the brother in the actual *koinonia* (life-together-in-love) of the church in which the Word is proclaimed and the sacraments administered. Thus the church is always a tangible, visible fellowship gathered by and about a living Lord, present to them in Word and sacraments. There is nothing "invisible" about such a church, although it is true that only God knows his own.

Hence a much better way of expressing that which is intended and undoubtedly must be taken into account is to say that the one church is always "hidden" and, therefore, always an object of faith. This rests upon the recognition of the fact that "love" and "faith" are never obvious, however necessary it is that they express themselves outwardly. The hidden life of love is nevertheless recognizable by its fruits.[3] There is no escaping this paradox of the Christian life. The hidden life of love is far too exacting for you to wear on your arm-length sleeve or betray by the sweetness of your breath. No outward profession, no matter how profuse, no ostentatious display of concern, even if it strips you to the skin or causes you to jump into the fire, will reveal with certainty whether or not there is "love" in the heart (I Corinthians 13). This, as Jesus says explicitly (Matthew 25), is reserved for the final judgment, when all the secrets of the heart will be revealed and each deed stand in its true worth and the cup of cold water given in Jesus' name shine like a precious jewel. Therefore, who the true believers are is always "hidden," but hidden in an actual *koinonia*

[2] Cf. Melanchthon in the Apology, Jacobs, *Book of Concord,* p. 165.
[3] Kierkegaard, *Works of Love* (Princeton: Princeton University Press, 1949).

of the church that is knit together by a love that cannot fail to raise the cry, "Behold, how they love one another!" No one, therefore, can smugly console himself with the notion of the "invisible" church. Every actual church must operate on the faith-conviction that it is the true church, that in it the will of God is finding expression, and, if it differs from another church also claiming to be the true church, then this is the call to self-examination, to repentance, to a fresh turning to God's Word in renewed efforts to remove this contradiction.

THE UNITY OF THE CHURCH IN WORD AND SACRAMENT

This takes us back to the original question as to what is and what is not essential to unity. By working out from the center, from the liberating and unifying act of God in Christ, we have already come to the conclusion that the church is constituted by the proclamation of the gospel and the administration of the sacraments and by nothing else. Where the gospel is proclaimed there Christ is present in his grace. The "words" themselves are not magic, potent powers which in themselves can do anything. The "words" proclaim events and bear witness to what has happened and announce the presence of the living God in both judgment and grace. The "words" are, therefore, the media and the "masks" in and through which Christ himself is present. The invitation the preacher gives, the judgment he pronounces, the forgiveness he proclaims are not his but God's. Here again is the "mediated immediacy" (John Baillie's phrase) of the "hidden" God, who is hidden in the medium but not thereby removed from the immediate encounter.

This is at the same time the repudiation of the notion that God, in his gracious disposition as the God who takes man's sin upon himself and in so doing really liberates and unites, could come to man somehow apart from *this* Word that proclaims *this* good news. This would be the denial of the very fact of revelation at a time and place and the necessity of carrying this good news from land to land. It would be the denial of that *koinonia* of the church in which every man is dependent upon the brother. This was Luther's stricture with those who claimed to have a direct wire to God and could therefore bypass the Word mediated by the brother, while nevertheless they belied themselves by trying to win converts through the Word. If you can find the gracious God by going into the silence or contemplating your navel squatting under the bo-tree, then you are not dependent upon that decisive act of liberation and unification which happened once and for all and now is made available in the proclamation of the Word and administration of the sacraments.[4]

Now quite obviously, if Christ as liberator and unifier is to be present and acting in the proclaimed Word and in the sacramental Word, then in both instances the proclamation must be right, it must say the right thing. Then this does make central and decisive the pure proclamation of the gospel and the administration of the sacraments in harmony with that gospel. Obviously, if a learned man in an academic gown with chevrons on his sleeves gets up and offers "ideals" to strive for and "universal principles" to be followed, or a code of laws to be obeyed, or, worse yet, invites you to join in a quest for a liberator who has not yet been discovered as physicians are still looking for a cancer cure, instead of proclaiming the Christ who *has* come, then the church can be neither constituted nor nurtured, and Christ cannot be present in a proclamation which does not proclaim his presence. Or if, in the administration of the sacrament of baptism—even though the formula be used—the public explanation of the act explicitly denies that this is incorporation into fellowship with the triune God and, therefore, a baptism into Christ's death and a rising with him to newness of life in his body, the church, but is only a sentimental, innocuous ceremony to show the worth God places upon little

[4] To show that this is not a peculiar Lutheran emphasis, see the fine statement in S. F. Allison, *The Fulness of Christ* (London: Society For Promoting Christian Knowledge, 1950), pp. 31, 32.

innocent children, then, although you cannot question the validity of the baptism without repeating the Donatist heresy, you do have to raise the question as to whether the church is present in and through such a proclamation, if you are not going to ascribe *ex opere operato* efficacy to the repetition of a formula.

Or, with respect to the Holy Communion, even if a man most solemnly repeats the words of institution and then states explicitly that Jesus was a man like others also and that in this meal of fellowship we dedicate ourselves to his kind and gentle spirit, although you can by no means question the presence of Christ in such a celebration, you cannot assert that the church is by this proclamation nourished and edified. The gracious presence of Christ would in such case be the judging Christ and the body and blood would be received as a judgment upon them. [5]

So it seems to me that there is no escaping this conclusion that everything depends upon the right proclamation of the gospel and the administration of the sacraments in harmony with it so that the proclamation makes clear that what happens in the sacrament is exactly that which the gospel proclaims. If the sacrament, therefore, is proclaimed to be anything other than the Word itself, it is the gospel itself that is distorted and perverted.

WORD AND SACRAMENTS, THE SOLE MARKS OF THE CHURCH

This is the Lutheran emphasis upon the *sole* and sufficient efficacy of the Word, which means in this case the actual proclamation and not the mere repetition of a formula nor does it in this instance refer to the Bible. There is a sense in which one must also speak of the sole and sufficient efficacy of the Bible, but this is because in it we have that selfsame, all-sufficient, efficacious gospel to which the Bible is the final and authoritative witness. Hence, Word and sacrament are the sole constitutive factors of the church and the sole "marks" of the church by which the church is recog-

[5] See also *The Fulness of Christ*, pp. 32-33.

nizable as present. "Faith" in the heart is not discernible but a proclamation is, and it can be checked with the witness of the Bible and the witness of the church through the years. Common rites and ceremonies cannot make evident the presence of the one church if the proclamation makes it quite evident that these rites are variously interpreted and understood. An external succession in the episcopacy cannot do this, if the one who stands in the right external continuity does not actually stand in the continuity of the proclamation of the only liberating and uniting Christ. An outward manner of life cannot be the distinguishing mark either, because, as already stated, the love that is hidden in the heart cannot be made explicit in the deed. The history of the church shows clearly that whenever men have tried to "clean house" and to identify the church solely from the manner of life of the believers, Christianity has been reduced to a code morality inescapably cut down to man's size. The very heart of the gospel proclamation is that the church is for sinners who find acceptance and fellowship there in spite of their sins.

Thus it is the gospel that remains the true "mark" of the church and not the degree of respectability of the members or their conformity to accepted patterns of behavior. Perhaps if this had been more unequivocally proclaimed we would not have the sorry spectacle of segregated churches and downtown clubs to which suburbanites motor on a Sunday morning in order to meet their friends. Moreover, the unpredictable behavior of the one freed from the law and free to love will always continue to be an offense to the legalists because the church sets no rigid patterns of behavior but allows love to respond freely to the moment's need.

Much more disconcerting than that outward disunity of organization is the fact of inner discord, the fact that you do not in Christendom everywhere hear the same liberating and uniting gospel proclaimed. It is this that becomes the wrong kind of "offense" to the non-Christian world. Instead of being at all times "offended" by the same proclamation of the stumbling block and foolishness of the cross, men are offended at the multiplicity of the proclamation. What difference would it make if there were four churches on four corners, each with different liturgies and outward trappings, if only you could go into each one and there hear in your own tongue, which speaks to your heart, the same glad, good news. It was not a tragedy, therefore, that as long as people did not really understand a foreign tongue they should have remained separate in the interests of hearing the gospel; the proclamation of the one gospel in six languages does not destroy the unity of the church as does the proclamation of six different "gospels" in one and the same language. The tragedy lies not in the multiplicity of church organizations but in the multiplicity of panaceas peddled by pontifical prophets, all shouting their contradictory, "Lo, here is Christ, and lo, there."

Moreover, it should also be clear that when churches openly state their disagreement there is not as much cause for offense as there is if there is a claim of being united which is then denied in the actual proclamation. Men cannot possibly choose which of the denominations they will choose to join when there is no agreement about what they stand for. The church must make up its mind as to what it is that it is offering to the world. And the only way to do this is to discuss it and to came to some agreement, *prior* to uniting rather than uniting and then working at cross-purposes and creating confusion worse confounded. It is by no means confusing if you know in advance that two churches do not agree and are prepared for it, but it is devastating if there is the bold claim of agreement and then you hear quite contradictory proclamations and meet quite contradictory practice that flows directly out of the contradictory proclamation.

The true unity of the church consists in the unity of Word and sacraments, which constitute the sole "marks" of the church. This is expressed in Article VII of the Augsburg Confession by the words "for the true unity of the church it is enough to agree concerning the proclamation of the gospel and the administration of the sacraments."

WHAT IS THE "SATIS EST" OF ARTICLE VII?

Something more, however, needs to be said about this *satis est* (it is sufficient). How much agreement must there be, how much leeway can you allow, where do you draw the line between what is essential and not essential?

Before an answer is given a few preliminary assertions are necessary, even though they involve a repetition of what has already been said: 1) The actual faith-relationship to the living Christ of the entire man in his existence is essential for being in the church. Being a Christian does not mean a mere top-of-the-head acceptance of certain doctrines or even putting one's trust in those doctrines as doctrines. It means, as we have said, an actual liberation and unification by means of a transformation of existence in the encounter with the love of God in the living Christ.

2) This transformation of existence and incorporation into the body of Christ is not possible without the right proclamation of the gospel and the attendant word of personal address and call to decision. This word is addressed to the entire person in his existence and must be intelligible and clearly distinguishable from false alternatives so that a person may as a person respond in either "faith" or "offense" to the absolute claim which he here recognizes to be made upon him. He is not to be seduced into the church by some kind of atmosphere or by the coercion of mass media of communication or any other devices that obscure the clearly understood call to a decision to forsake other lords and surrender to this one.

3) While the formulation and acceptance of doctrine is not to be equated with the personal faith-relationship, it is most certainly inseparable from it. The events of the gospel are inseparable from the doctrines which state what is believed and refute false alternatives. While the biblical record is not just a compendium

of doctrines or truths but the witness to certain events, it is as such a witness replete with the doctrines which the transformed believers affirmed and which distinguished them from their pagan neighbors.

4) Such doctrinal formulations are always addressed to a situation and, therefore, are meaningful only in that context. You understand Paul's Letter to the Galatians only in the light of the Judaizing insistence upon the keeping of the law and in the light of Paul's whole background, mode of thinking, environment. You understand John's Gospel only in the light of a Gnostic denial of the coming of very God into the flesh, Matthew's Gospel only in the light of his concern to convince fellow-Jews of the fulfilment of prophecy, Mark's Gospel only in the light of his attempt to impress the practical Romans, and so forth. The same is true of all creedal affirmations and confessions and all theologies which are always addressed to a situation and are understood only in the light of that situation.

5) Though the essential human situation remains the same, the actual situations of men vary considerably at different times and places. Ways of thinking vary, advances are made in the various fields of knowledge; the whole manner of living will accentuate different problems at different times. To each situation the gospel must be made relevant and all the implications of the gospel worked out in opposition to prevailing alternatives.

6) There can be no fixation of theology in a system adequate for all times, stated precisely thus and so, once and for all. This is the mistake of Thomism, which fixates once and for all in Aristotelian categories the process of man's progress toward the realization of his true end. For good or ill, it was with this "system" Luther broke, while a later orthodoxy returned to it and thus destroyed the existential character of the affirmations of faith.

7) A "system" of theology is, therefore, to be understood as something quite different from a philosophical, rationally coherent system of truths, or an organized system of doctrines simply derived from the Bible as the compendium of such doctrines and

then organized in accordance with some principle. Rather, there is to be a consistent understanding of the gospel and a working out of all its implications. This means the working out of an organic whole in terms of a dominant motif which will give cast and color and direction and quality to the whole. It is a matter of beginning at the center, as we are trying to do in this presentation, and then allowing that really to be determinative, and letting it radiate into every direction and permeate every detail.

8) Unity of faith, *i.e.* the unity of those who are one in Christ, must find expression in a commonly accepted "system of theology" thus defined. It is not a matter of pious feeling but of precise doctrinal expression which clearly reveals the basic understanding of how the right God-relationship is established and maintained.

9) Such unity of faith is, however, not achieved once and for all by agreement upon one doctrinal system fixated for all times in precisely those terms. This would be confusing the word of man and the word of God, a man-made theology with the actual, divine self-impartation. This would make man the master who has God boxed up in these formulations and would be a denial of justification by faith.

10) Unity of faith, therefore, must, in each generation become apparent anew as men wrestle with God's word to hear and understand what he is saying. Whether or not they are actually one in faith will become apparent to men only as they honestly wrestle with contemporary problems and try to work out all the implications of their understanding of the gospel in the contemporary situation.

11) When agreement is reached and only after this agreement is reached can and must there be full church fellowship. Such agreement is not created by the common confession, but the common confession is the expression of the agreement and is the *sine qua non* of church fellowship.

12) The creeds and confessions of the past are to be understood as testimonies to an actually existing unity of faith on the part of all

who subscribed to the creed or confession. If anyone subscribes to the same creeds today, he can do so in oneness with that confession only if he puts himself back into that context.

13) Hence the *satis est* of Article VII, which is the sole condition of the true unity of the church, is not a 100 per cent agreement, or for that matter any kind of quantitative agreement upon a specifiable sum of separate doctrines. It is, first of all, a qualitative matter of the total orientation and as such it means full and wholehearted agreement on a certain total, qualitative understanding of the gospel, *i.e.* of how the right God-relation and with it the right man-to-man relation is established and maintained. This will allow nothing to be a matter of indifference in so far as it is really related to the center and is part of the total orientation. [6]

It is with this issue particularly that Lutherans must come to grips because the greatest barrier to fellowship has been precisely this insistence upon a quantitative degree of acceptance of a once-and-for-all fixated body of doctrine, an insistence which I hold to be out of harmony with the confessional position of the Lutheran Church. The writers of the Augsburg Confession could not have had in mind adherence to a system of doctrine which at that time had not yet been formulated. They clearly had in mind such a proclamation of the gospel which was in harmony with their understanding of the biblical witness as they were setting it forth in their confession, always allowing that this confession was again to be tested by God's Word itself.

One attitude insists upon a 100 per cent agreement on all doctrines clearly taught in the Scriptures and thus allows no so-called "open questions." Either, they say, the Scriptures are not clear, and then you cannot make it a matter of doctrine one way or the other, or else the Scriptures are quite clear and then the matter is settled once and for all, and so there are no "open questions." There are, of course, admitted to be *adiaphora,* matters of clear indifference, which do not involve a doctrinal stand. However, such *adiaphora*

[6] See C. P. Krauth, *op. cit.,* p. 23.

may at any time take on a confessional status, if they are insisted upon and no longer held to be a matter of indifference.[7]

Those opposed to the above orientation, however, are no better off when they allow for "open questions" on the same basis of a specifiable number of biblical doctrines, on 85 per cent of which, let us say, there must be agreement, while on 15 per cent of them you have an option. There is a valid insight into the wholeness of the gospel which objects to this kind of fragmentization. No doctrine is unessential if it is really an integral part of the whole.

Therefore, what is needed is a different orientation which holds to the *sola scriptura,* not in terms of propositional truth and a compendium of doctrines, but as the witness to God's great deeds of redemption, which must be understood as a qualitative whole from the center in Christ. This is taking seriously the *analogia fidei.*

What we have tried to establish is this: If the oneness of the church, which is God's gift and actually exists in the one, holy, catholic, apostolic church, is also to find outward expression in full church fellowship, then this can be done only on the basis of agreement on the gospel or, in other words, on the basis of doctrinal agreement. "Doctrine" in this case is not a "bad" word, but means simply the clear and articulate expression of what the good news actually is, not as a world-view, but as God's own answer to the predicament of man in his existence. Such doctrinal agreement is, however, not to mean a quantitative degree of agreement on an aggregate of a specifiable number of doctrines, some of which are essential and others peripheral. It is rather a matter of a total orientation, an organic whole permeated by a dominant motif, in the answer that is given to the basic question of life as to how the God-relation is established and maintained. The *agape, eros,* and *nomos* motifs do then present an exhaustive enumeration of possibilities. Making central the doctrine of justification by grace alone, for Christ's sake through faith, only means making the *agape* motif dominant and giving both *eros* and *nomos* their proper subordinate

[7] See Formula of Concord X.

place in harmony with this dominance. This, in typically Lutheran terms, means the proper distinction between law and gospel. This central understanding will determine everything else. It will determine the *sola scriptura,* because it makes this center central.

It determines the meaning you give to the ecumenical creeds (for these are accepted by Roman Catholics and Protestants alike with the greatest diversity of interpretation), what you say about the sacraments, how you regard the ministry, how you describe the Christian life, what you say about the relations between state and church, and so forth. The gospel, of course, is what it is and we can never be cocksure that our theology or our proclamation (witness) does full justice to it. Thus, the confessions do not make the acceptance of a particular theology precisely so formulated the *conditio sine qua non* of unity. Hence, even within a confessional church there must continue to be the wrestling for the right proclamation of the gospel. Every preacher who mounts the pulpit from which he is not to dispense his own wisdom as a village sage but to announce the word of God, every teacher who means not merely to assist his pupil like a midwife in giving birth to his own ideas but really to beget the truth in him, every householder who means to minister as a priest to those God has put nearest to him, every brother who speaks to another to console him at a moment when all other helpers fail, is challenged on this view to examine again and again whether or not he is rightly proclaiming the gospel. And *a fortiore* every church, when it comes to make common cause with another group from which it has in the past been separated because of what were then considered vital differences in the central understanding of the gospel, must ask itself whether these differences which were once considered vital still exist or have actually been overcome, or whether they were not misunderstandings in the first place. Only if some understanding is reached can there be full fellowship. [8]

[8] See the different point of view presented by W. E. Garrison in *The Third World Conference on Faith and Order* (London: SCM, 1953), p. 185.

THE QUESTION OF LUTHERAN UNITY

If to the true unity of the church it is enough to agree concerning the right proclamation of the gospel and the administration of the sacraments in harmony therewith, (this is the position to which all Lutherans subscribe), then this raises the all-important question of Lutheran unity. Certainly there is in a sense a prior obligation to Lutheran unity which takes precedence over unity with others who do not subscribe to the same confession, but then we can, in church political interests, make no concessions here either. What is sauce for the goose is also sauce for the gander. If the actual proclamation of the gospel is primary and not just a nominal subscription to a forgotten historical document, then Lutherans too must assure themselves that they are actually holding and proclaiming the same thing.

The first thing on which there should be agreement is the nature of the confessional subscription, to which we shall return in the next chapter. Briefly it is this: The creeds and confessions mark certain historical points as watersheds which in a specific historical situation were decisive and determined a definite parting of the ways, *e.g.* Arianism *vs.* Athanasius and Nicene Christianity, and later the various Protestant confessions as over against the Enthusiasts (fully recognizing the need today to listen to what the Pentecostals have to say), the Zwinglians, the Calvinists.

As we put ourselves back into a past century and understand the issues as the fathers faced them, we must choose where we will stand. This demands a parting of the ways. Here is a watershed. Unless and until some orientation *(Fragestellung)* can be found from which the difficulties can be overcome, there will have to be a choice. You can't carry water on both shoulders. This, then, is what confessional subscription means: On all the issues raised by the confessions, as they still recur today and where no additional light from the Scriptures has been thrown upon them, we choose to stand where the confessions stand. This is the abiding value of the confession (see next chapter) which at the same time gives freedom for continuing reform.

It would be well to call to the attention again of all the Lutheran bodies what was set forth by the United Lutheran Church in 1934 in the Savannah Resolution:

"We recognize as Evangelical Lutherans all Christian groups which accept the Holy Scriptures as the only rule and standard for faith and life, by which all doctrines are to be judged, and who sincerely receive the historic Confessions of the Lutheran Church (especially the Unaltered Augsburg Confession) as a witness of the truth and a presentation of the correct understanding of our predecessors;[9] *and we set up no other standards or tests of Lutheranism apart from them or alongside of them.*

"We believe that the Confessions are to be interpreted in their historical context, not as a law or as a system of theology, but as 'a witness and declaration of faith as to how the Holy Scriptures were understood and explained on the matters in controversy within the Church of God by those who then lived.'[10]

"Inasmuch as our now-separated Lutheran Church bodies all subscribe these same confessions, it is our sincere belief that we already possess a firm basis on which to unite in one Lutheran Church in America and that there is no doctrinal reason why such a union should not come to pass. We believe that it would have God's blessing and we pray that He will grant to all of us the wisdom, the courage and the patience to accomplish it."[11]

This should settle the question as to the manner in which the confessions are to be subscribed since the confessions themselves demand to be understood in their context. Furthermore, if we trust one another in the sincerity of our confessional subscription, then no other tests of Lutheranism can very well be demanded and we ought to be able to proceed to the practical questions of actual

[9] *Formula of Concord,* Part II, ed. C. M. Jacobs, p. 538.
[10] *Ibid.,* Part I, p. 492.
[11] Lee, *Doctrinal Declaration* (St. Louis: 1939), p. 59f.

union. The United Lutheran Church in America, which is regarded as the most liberal of the Lutheran bodies, significantly pledges its ministry not only to the Augsburg Confession but to the entire Book of Concord, and it can do so with good conscience since it sees them as a qualitative whole rather than as an aggregate.

But it does not follow that this would mean the end of all theological discussion. Lip service to a confession of the past, while allowing a diversity of interpretation, is not a sufficient basis for agreement. If the confessions of the sixteenth century really make the right proclamation of the gospel central, then this demands theological discussion and self-examination to determine if this is really so. This will be done on the basis of mutual trust both as intending to be faithful to the confessions and of acceptance, assuming that we do agree until that disagreement really becomes apparent. If one church demands that disciplinary action be taken against those in other church bodies who in their practice do not conform to the official position of the church, then this is a two-edged sword. Is it, *e.g.*, in harmony with the confessional position of the Lutheran Church to demand that the sacrament be celebrated every Sunday, or to tell a person that he cannot be accepted as taking his Christianity seriously if he is unwilling to tithe, and, if not, what disciplinary action is the church taking against those who so assert? Or, what kind of casuistry is it which allows lodge members to come to the Lord's Supper but refuses them voting membership in the church? Since when does voting membership in an organization take precedence over participation in the body and blood of Christ?

If it is loyalty to the truth of the gospel alone that matters then no one should be spared, least of all he who claims to hold the same confession. But the truth must always be spoken in love.

We must honestly face the fact that the really burning issues among us as Lutherans today are the attitude toward the word of God, the nature of confessional subscription, so-called unionism and the question of pulpit and altar fellowship, and the lodge question especially in so far as it concerns pastors belonging to lodges. Beyond that, new problems are arising, particularly those raised by the high-church movement and the conception of the relation between Word and sacrament. These are live and vital issues which strike at the heart of the gospel and what the Reformation was all about. Unless we are willing to continue to wrestle with these problems theologically, there can be no health in the church. There can be no other ultimate criterion except a theological one on the basis of God's word. What we are proposing, therefore, is that the same rule should apply to inter-Lutheran relations as to interdenominational ones. We must together wrestle for an actual consensus in the way described, trying always to see everything from the center. Only in so far as we do this are we true to the heritage of the Reformation. Of course, if anyone really believes that the Reformers were basically wrong or that what you believe and what kind of a gospel you proclaim doesn't really matter, and that the last thing Christian pastors and people should be concerned about is theology, then such a one is in the wrong camp.

PULPIT AND ALTAR FELLOWSHIP

If agreement on the gospel as described is the basis of full church fellowship, what shall we then say about the vexing question of pulpit and altar fellowship?

On the view here presented, altar fellowship is not the first step on the way to unity, but the expression of the unity which has previously found expression in a common confession. The sacrament of the altar differs from the sacrament of baptism in that while baptism stands at the beginning of the life of the Christian as the initial act of God's liberation and unification, the sacrament of the altar is God's repeated act of liberation and unification by means of which the believer is strengthened in his relation to God and the neighbor.

Here is the visible expression of the "hidden" church expressing the totality of the relationship in the most intimate *koinonia* of body, soul and spirit *(totus homo)* which draws all the common stuff of life into it (the bread and the wine). It never—not by the wildest stretch of the imagination—would have occurred to the first Christians to open the closed circle of this redeemed fellowship to those who did not know what it was all about and had not themselves been apprehended. The celebration of this "mystery" was reserved for those "who discerned the Lord's body," who were able to examine themselves and would *so* eat and would not desecrate this holy, saving presence and this *koinonia* of the body of Christ by their unseemly behavior (I Corinthians 10:11). How could this fellowship simply be opened to all who in some vague way are impressed by the trappings and feel all "ooshy" inside, because there are subtly changing neon lights, tremulous organ music and cherub choirs, or incense, the jingling of bells, the swish of garments, the rhythmic patter of feet up and down the altar steps, and mysterious motions and mumbled mumbo jumbo?

This is not a "mystic" experience in which those who have been too much belabored by preaching and too much taxed by thinking may at last find refuge in a bath of feeling. It is either mysticism, and then you can dispense with Bethlehem and Calvary and Easter morn, or else the Word, and then the risen Lord himself meets you and greets you as he did "Mary" in the garden and imparts himself to you. You do not in that moment lose consciousness or go into a trance. Nowhere must you be more awake, more conscious of what is going on, more stabbed to the quick with the awareness of the self in the pain of guilt and joy of acceptance, more keenly aware of who accepts you and at what price of suffering this acceptance was made possible, more actively joined to the brother with whom one is here leveled to the true equality of common sinfulness and common belovedness, than here in this sacrament. How then shall this sacrament be "opened" to any but those who have been informed and have made the decision and been received into this fellowship and are now consciously nurtured in it not by a thingified infusion of inert substances or powers of grace but by the self-impartation of the gracious God in an all-inclusive relation?

At present there are still two contradictory opinions in the church: the opinion of those who would use the communion as a device to create unity, and the opinion of those who feel that the communion should be the outward expression of an existing unity. It is with the latter group that we have taken our stand for what we believe to be valid reasons, from the center of the gospel itself. But this still needs further qualification.

We have said that the church is the "hidden" church and that it exists wherever the gospel is rightly proclaimed and the sacraments administered in harmony with that gospel. It is not necessary, therefore, that there be communion across the lines of existing denominations in order thereby to create unity, because this unity already exists, even though there are so many different altars. The outward expression of the existing unity is always there in the "marks" of the church which are the right proclamation of the gospel and the administration of the sacraments in harmony therewith. Each denomination, therefore, will be bound to safeguard its altar for those who share the same understanding of the gospel and the sacraments. The inability, for conscience' sake, to join with others at the altar will be the constant spur to find "doctrinal unity." It is wrong to make a pretense of unity at the altar which does not in fact exist. If there are differences in the understanding of the gospel—and no other differences on this view matter—which justify a separate denomination, then how can this be contradicted at the altar? If they can commune together at the same altar, then remaining in a separate denomination is unjustified. If we should feel that we can commune at a Roman Catholic altar, then we have no right not to return to Rome. And the same is true also of the various Protestant altars. This leads us to reaffirm the Galesburg Rule, provided only it is applied in its entirety as it was originally adopted at Akron in 1872, to wit:

"The *rule* is, Lutheran pulpits are for Lutheran ministers only, Lutheran altars are for Lutheran communicants only.

"The exceptions to the rule belong to the sphere of privilege, not of right.

"The determination of the exceptions is to be made in consonance with those principles by the conscientious judgment of the pastors as the cases arise." [12]

Insofar as this applies to the pulpit it most certainly is the sacred obligation of the church to safeguard its proclamation and, therefore, not to open its pulpit to every peddler of panaceas. This is as basic as the basic assumption of this whole series that in the ecumenical church the concern for the truth must be primary. In 1889 (General Council convention, Pittsburgh) it was resolved that "the purity of the pulpit should be guarded with the most conscientious care and that no man shall be admitted to our pulpits, *whether of the Lutheran name or any other,* of whom there is just reason to doubt whether he will preach the pure truth of God's Word as taught in the Confessions of our Church." Granted that all hinges upon how the phrase, "the pure truth of God's Word taught in the Confessions . . . " is understood (on that we have tried to throw some light by pointing to the qualitative wholeness of the understanding of the gospel dominated by one basic motif), as long as Christianity claims to possess the one true gospel, which it is obligated to preach to all the world in every time and place in radical correction of all religions, there should be no question as to the basic soundness of this position, not only among Lutherans but among all members of Christ's church who are really concerned about the gospel as they are constrained to proclaim it.

The pulpit is not a lecture platform but a place of proclamation endowed with the authority not indeed of learning or of some external succession, but of the Word itself that is proclaimed there and what safeguards can be set up certainly must be set up. We have

[12] See Minutes of the Sixth Convention of the General Convention of the General Council in Akron, 1872, pp. 46-47.

wandered very far from a concern for what is really important when we take the utmost precaution that no unordained man should ever administer or even assist at the sacrament and then allow high-school lads with no theological training and no understanding of the gospel whatever to supply pulpits and positively to proclaim the most shocking heresy. Unless a man had St. Vitus dance, he could not do much harm assisting at the communion, but who will estimate the harm done by the teen-age Elvis Presley pulpiteer?

But taking seriously the safeguarding of the pulpit already points to *the privilege and indeed the obligation of exercising at all times a selective fellowship, even on occasions where fellow-Lutherans are concerned.* Every pastor and congregation must be allowed this freedom both to extend and withhold a privilege and, if it is abused, *abusus non tollit usum.* If there are abuses such as really compromise the gospel, then some kind of disciplinary action certainly ought to be taken, provided it really begins with proper personal counseling, and is always done in love. This would appear to me to give every man the full leeway the present confused situation demands. There is actually often—and we might as well honestly face this—a much better understanding among non-Lutherans of the explicitly Lutheran confessional position in its grasp of the richness, fulness, and profundity of the gospel, than among some of those who subscribe the confessions. And this is precisely on those points we say we cherish, as for example, *sola scriptura, sola gratia, sola fide,* the real presence in the sacrament, the *simul justus et peccator,* the doctrines of the universal priesthood and the vocation. It is high time that we move in both directions, a proper safeguarding of the pulpit together with a judicious opening of it in the interests of the proclamation of the truth. This is no vindication of the kind of "unionism" in which the gospel and the confessional loyalty of the church are compromised.

As for altar fellowship, the same rule should apply, with the possibility always of exceptions being granted as a privilege and not as a right. In the Lutheran Church admission to the Lord's Supper is granted to its own members only after confirmation, on the basis of the conviction that participation in this sacrament presupposes a certain maturity, a certain amount of instruction, and a conscious awareness of what happens in the sacrament. If this is proper and in harmony with the nature of the sacrament and not an undue restriction of the Lord's table, then it is very inconsistent for a congregation to allow to the member of another church, which may require no instruction, a privilege not granted to its own membership. As we have said, the unity of the one church of Christ is neither destroyed if all do not commune at the same altar nor established if they do. The nurture of the body of Christ depends certainly not upon an *ex opere operato* reception of the sacrament but upon the maintenance of the right personal relationship. Christ did not go about offering a sacrament to all and sundry whether they understood what it was all about or not. He went into the homes of sinners, and by word and deed elicited the responses of humble faith. To such as he had chosen he gave the bread and the wine, and in the enlightenment of the Holy Spirit after his resurrection and ascension they knew what this meant. Shall we then open this table to such as have no awareness that such an enlightenment and transformation are even necessary? Anyone who has any awareness of the babel of cults and the degeneracy of preaching on the American scene and the ignorance and illiteracy of most people who go regularly to church without knowing the rudiments of Christian doctrine, ought to think twice before he "opens" the altar to all and sundry. The place to begin is certainly not with a sentimental broadmindedness about the altar (as though Christianity did not make the most exacting demands) but with better instruction as to what the gospel really is and the radical transformation of life it requires. It is the Lord's Supper and *not ours;* and it is not we who set up the restriction, but the Lord himself who calls men out of the world into his kingdom. Greater frequency of communion with the tendency of cheapening it and making it routine and deadly might better give way to taking the communion more seriously and preparing for it more earnestly and participating in it more joyfully. All reform of sacramental practice—like all reform—must issue from a deepening understanding and appreciation of the gospel itself. So the rule in my opinion should stand, precisely because it allows for the exceptions in our confused day.

LODGE MEMBERSHIP

As for the lodge question, it would seem that the only solution is that proposed by none less than C. F. W. Walther [13] as well as in the Washington Declaration (ULCA, 1920), namely, to witness constructively to the gospel and to condemn unequivocally whatever the gospel condemns, letting the chips fall where they may, but exercising patience and proper pastoral care *(Seelsorge)* in a matter of conscience. Where pastors themselves are involved, it would seem that all hinges on whether or not they give a clear and unequivocal witness to the gospel in faithfulness to the doctrinal position of the church. It is on this score they should be examined and then a clear understanding of the gospel will rule out affiliation with any definitely anti-Christian group or any compromise of the minister's position as the shepherd of his flock by a special relation to a certain group or a vow of secrecy that must conflict with the "openness" which the Christian *koinonia* demands. If a housecleaning is demanded as the precondition of Lutheran unity, then it will have to be on both sides of the fence. Inconsistencies between the official position and the actual practice will have to be removed all the way around. At this point all bodies concerned are in one way or another vulnerable. In lieu of that we shall have to recognize our mutual fallibility and trust one another in the sincerity of our adherence to a common confession and in our efforts to bring the saving gospel without compromise to all. The central emphasis must be always where we have put it on the right proclamation

[13] See Conrad Bergendoff, *The Doctrine of the Church in American Lutheranism.* (Philadelphia: Muhlenberg Press, 1956).

of the gospel which alone can bring the right conduct and practice in its wake. On that score we must all constantly hold ourselves under scrutiny.

THE ECUMENICAL MOVEMENT

Finally there is the question of participation in the ecumenical movement to which all members of the Lutheran World Federation are pledged. Here the whole thrust presented in the initial chapter should come into its own. By the common consent of the members of the World Council, the peculiar contribution of the Lutheran Church has been the insistence upon the *consensus de doctrina* as the prerequisite for full fellowship, while nevertheless remaining open to the others. This means the insistence upon the kind of qualitative understanding of the whole gospel from the center in Christ here presented. Paraphrasing the study document for the assembly, the Lutheran Church does not presume that it alone is the true church—Article VII of the Augsburg Confession forbids such a view—but its task is to point the whole church and all church bodies to the true evangelical structure of the church, and to what is essential and what is not. It is, therefore, a sacred trust with which the Lutheran Church is charged, with her peculiar gifts and responsibilities, to take an active part in the ecumenical movement and to strive to contribute to making more visible the already existing unity of the one true church, but to do so without compromise of the gospel as it understands it. Hence we cannot say that the experience of oneness across the lines of existing denominations is sufficient and that we can stop here and just co-operate in common tasks. Beyond this we must strive for full fellowship and unity in the gospel. Because of this sense of ecumenical responsibility, teachings which endanger the faith and disturb and destroy the church must be branded as heresy, and such teachings must be countered by the Word of God itself.

Above all, the Lutheran Church is bound together with others in a positive and constructive way, under the Word of God, to wrestle for true unity and agreement with respect to the right proclamation of the gospel. In so doing there must be no shadow-boxing about its own confession which must be put fully to the test and must always be proved with the touchstone of Scriptures, so that there is real openness to learn from others. Whenever there is real consensus with others, then recognition must be granted and full church fellowship practiced. It is never, however, to be assumed that organizational unity is an end in itself. Infinitely more important than a monolithic church structure which straitjackets and confines is freedom for the gospel to have its way and to build for itself whatever structures shall further its cause.

We have risen to a defense of Article VII of the Augsburg Confession. To be sure the Lutheran Church cannot be proud of its record, but this is not the fault of Article VII. The issues raised there must first be settled. Is anything else to be essential to the church beside the right proclamation of the gospel and such an administration of the sacraments as is in harmony with it? With what else do we propose to build the church? With gimmicks and brass bands and shots in the arm? What is there that will meet man's existential need if not the right proclamation of the gospel which all of us must always be straitened to proclaim?

It seems to me there is no conception of the church which will give it greater flexibility than this. Nothing matters really—no altar, no vestments, no choir, no cute little cherub putting out the light of God for another week, no starched patterns of congregational life, no hard and fast dogmas fixated in outmoded categories —*nothing matters but that the gospel be rightly proclaimed and all its implications spelled out for all of life, that it be taken seriously what it means that the Word was made flesh and dwelt among us in order that men might be restored to their true humanity and so minister to each other in a universal priesthood of love.*

IV

The Freedom to Reform the Church

My intention in this chapter is to try to describe the tension between freedom and bondage in a church that is bound by a confession which liberates. The thesis is that it is only in bondage to the Reformation and its understanding of the gospel that there is true freedom constantly to reform the church.

Today there are conflicting tendencies. The first feels that a confessional subscription is a millstone around the neck of progress. It binds you to outmoded formulations of a day that is past and makes it impossible to meet the needs of today. We must, therefore, get a fresh start, unhampered by the past confessions that once divided the church, a new orientation that will not have within it the seeds of past divisions.

The second, which is growing in intensity, represents a flight to security, to the irrevocableness of past decisions, to a closed and guaranteed system. So Protestants are viewing the Reformation itself with suspicion. To be a Protestant is to be a rampant individualist with no feeling for the church. Protestants are almost as bad as "existentialists" or "dialectical theologians." The Reformation was the unfortunate beginning of disunity and a chaotic confusion of tongues, lacking the continuity, solidarity, rationality and external splendor of "Mother Church." So there is this romantic looking backward to the lost paradise, the one, great, united church—which is, however, a fiction and never existed. What actually existed was a multiplicity of the most diverse views held together by an external organization and even this organizational unity was split (*e.g.* East against West).

It is time, therefore, to speak a most energetic "yes" to the Reformation in such a way that a proper security is found but with all the false props knocked out and with the freedom for ongoing reformation and renewal preserved.

NO NEW CHURCH

It is necessary, first of all, to say that the Reformation did not found a new church. Article VII of the Augsburg Confession emphatically asserts the continuity of the church: "*Una sancta ecclesia perpetuo mansura sit.*" In the very nature of what the church is there cannot ever be a break in the historic continuity of the church, *i.e.* an interval of time in which there is no church upon the earth. No new church, therefore, came into being at the time of the Reformation, nor did the apostolic church after an interval of nonexistence emerge again. What happened was that the "hidden" church which was there all the time, where the living Christ was in Word and sacrament, took on a new lease of life. A *kairos* in the life of the church resulted in a renewal of life. The Reformation came not from the changing of externals, but from a fresh understanding of the gospel and its clear and unequivocal proclamation. The one holy, catholic, apostolic church broke through where the gospel alone, the Word of God alone, Christ alone in his gracious coming to man was the sole and supreme Lord and Judge (Galatians 2:3-5).

With this we are back with our main thesis, that it is Christ himself, in clear and unequivocal proclamation, who frees and unites all the members of his body in unbreakable continuity through both space and time, because the message must be brought in living persons from land to land and never drops straight from heaven. Luther, therefore, by no means destroyed the true unity of the church but only showed wherein it actually consists and what its basis is. No other criteria were to be set up, nothing except the gospel itself was to be the basis of acceptance into fellowship.

Our "yes" to the Reformation is, therefore, not at all confining or narrowing or restricting, but in the true sense liberating, because it shows where the church is bound and where, as the result of this binding, it is free; and far greater and more precious is the freedom than the bondage. Only to the law-free gospel in Christ does the Reformation commit us and to nothing else.

For theology and the proclamation of the church this means that we are not bound by the thought-forms, the categories, the peculiar expressions of a period, the current philosophies of a given time, but only to the gospel message itself which is at all times unchanging and, in fact, in a new and different situation must be expressed differently in order that it may say the same thing.[1]

It is particularly this which American Lutheranism needs to hear and it should listen in humility and calmness as this is being said, and not cry "heresy" when it does not recognize time-hallowed words, or when it is pointed out that there are certain blind spots which we ourselves fail to see but which are quite obvious to others. Anders Nygren has pointed to the pictures in the family album which never cease to amaze us. We could not possibly have looked like that, and yet we did, and we today will look just as ridiculous to the next generation. We never see our own faults and peculiarities until we get some perspective on them.

THE REPUDIATION OF SCHOLASTICISM

What is essentially involved, a fact which my teacher, Dr. J. Michael Reu, never failed to point out (although he himself did not follow suit) is that Luther broke completely with the categories of scholasticism in which the whole system which he attacked was cast. Of course he still used the same words, but chameleon-like these words took on a different color in the new context, dominated

[1] See the words of Bishop Ihmels, *Report of the Proceeding, Lutheran World Convention, Copenhagen, 1929,* p. 85; also Newbigin, *The Reunion of the Church,* pp. 137-38; 142; 146.

by a different motif, as present-day Luther research has shown.[2] He returned to a biblical orientation completely foreign to the scholastic orientation, and yet it was precisely to that orientation that seventeenth-century orthodoxists returned and while they wrestled nobly to do justice to the dynamic of the gospel, they nevertheless straitjacketed and imprisoned it. With ever finer and finer rational distinctions they tried their best to do justice to the mysteries of the faith and to safeguard them against heresy. But because the basic orientation of the philosophy with which they operated was wrong, it resulted in any number of the most fearful distortions. Nevertheless it cannot be denied that in many ways they served their time well, and we must gratefully and humbly recognize that their actual piety was better than their theology and even like the gospel itself burst through the prison house of the system into which it was cast. But if, today, American Lutherans insist on a doctrinal agreement in the terms of seventeenth-century orthodoxy and cry heresy at the slightest deviation, then all hope of American Lutheran unity is lost, to say nothing of rapport with world Lutheranism and the ecumenical movement.

It would take a whole textbook in dogmatics to work this out in detail and to try to do justice to the issues involved, but perhaps we can illustrate the point in one area. So, for example, the doctrine of God followed the pattern of the definition of other terms, classifying God in the class of personal beings and then distinguishing him from other members of this class by various attributes, such as absoluteness, aseity, holiness, and so forth, arriving at these attributes *via eminentiae, via negationis* and *via causalitatis.* This is boxing God up very neatly and, even if the anthropomorphisms are recognized as inadequate, the whole procedure cannot do justice to the living God, who in the Bible is not ever defined in this way,

[2] See, e.g. Watson, *Let God be God;* Carlson, *The Reinterpretation of Luther;* Rupp, *The Righteousness of God;* Prenter, *Spiritus Creator;* Nygren, *Agape and Eros;* Bainton, *Here I Stand;* Pelikan, *From Luther to Kierkegaard.* See Bibliography.

but only described in his actions in the most lordly, quite arbitrary, irrational, offensive, contradictory fashion. Once having boxed up God in the definition, it is the very devil to liberate him again.

Following the same pattern a distinction is made between the essence of God and his attributes. The essence of God is like the essence of chairness which you grasp with the mind and of which you are, therefore, the complete master. This essence remains as unchanging and unaffected by time as any abstract thought. In this essence the attributes inhere and from it they are detachable, at least some of them, without affecting the essence. So, for example, you can retain the idea of chairness, void of any particular attribute (accident) such as a particular color, or material, or shape, just so you retain the "essential" chair idea as distinguished from a couch, hassock, stool or other possible articles of furniture made to sit on. So also with God, the attributes inhere in the essence and, some of them at least, are detachable without thereby destroying the essence.

So far this might be comparatively harmless, as long as it is quite clear that the living God is not captured in this way; that he, in spite of the attempted definition, remains forever subject and only to be encountered, so to speak, face to face (even though in a "mask"). The moment you reduce him to these thoughts in your mind you lose the living God who confronts you, just as surely as you lose the living person confronting you the moment you reduce him to a definition, an abstract thought in your mind, abstracted from existence. But the trouble does not stop here, and there are all kinds of ramifications in such a system which is all of one piece, and, therefore, cannot be attacked piecemeal, accepted and rejected in part; it calls for an either-or.

Take, for example, the doctrine of the real presence in the Lord's Supper. This is a comparatively simple matter for Roman Catholics. The accidents of color, taste, and smell, and even of chemical composition of bread and wine remain, so that the elements still not only look, taste, and smell like bread and wine, but a chemical analysis of the transubstantiated bread and wine would reveal nothing except bread and wine, these all being accidents separable from the essence. In the "transubstantiation," the essences (or substances) of bread and wine have been replaced by the essences (or substances) of body and blood minus their peculiar accidents. So as a result you have substances of glorified body and blood completely disguised in accidents of bread and wine. On the premises, a neat rational explanation! But what has happened in the meantime to the confrontation with the living God? How absolutely foreign this is to anything which would have entered the mind of the Jew! And what in heaven's name would a modern chemist or physicist, who thinks in terms of relations where no essence is separable from its attributes, do with this kind of an explanation?

Now if a countering theology (seventeenth-century orthodoxy) adopts these same categories and in the same orientation simply substitutes "consubstantiation" for "transubstantiation," then certainly no advance is made, unless consubstantiation is really only a convienient word which, however, because is appears in a different context, means something quite different.

That the scholastic orientation prevailed is quite evident from the doctrines of the *communicatio idiomatum* and the *kenosis* which have played such an important role in the discussions of the real presence in the sacrament. The logic is exactly the same as that of the scholastics, although the intent is quite different. There are certain attributes, not really "essential" (sic!) to deity, of which God could divest himself without therefore ceasing to be God, just as the essences of body and blood are not tied to their accidents of smell, taste, and so forth. Among these divestible attributes are those of omniscience and omnipresence. When God became man in Christ he emptied himself (*kenosis,* exinanition) of these attributes of his majestic divinity and though he was still in essence God he was no longer either omniscient or omnipresent but limited in these respects like every other creature.

But this is now further complicated by the *communicatio idioma-*

tum.[3] This has to do with the hypostatic union of the two natures in the one person of Christ and the communication of the attributes of one nature to the other, again operating with separable attributes. (Just when this act of communication took place, whether prior to the incarnation or after is another neat problem with which we can't deal here, but which illustrates the refinements to which such a view has to be reduced.) The particular attribute which concerns us is omnipresence, which was communicated from the divine to the human nature at the incarnation, but then temporarily abandoned or not made use of in the *kenosis* during the state of humiliation, to be resumed again at the ascension and the return to the state of exaltation. So it is this which accounts for the "real" presence of the humanity of Jesus, *i.e.* the actual body and blood, though indeed glorified, in the sacrament of the altar, and keeps it from being a mere "spiritual" presence, that is, a presence somehow apart from this presence of the humanity. It was this argumentation which was used to answer the Calvinist notion that the body could by definition be only at one place and, therefore, was confined to the right hand of God in heaven. For Luther, however, the right hand of God was not a place but symbolized the exercise of the royal function of rule.

Since it is precisely the Lutheran doctrine of the real presence which has played such a tremendous role in keeping Lutherans apart in efforts at reunion, it is well that this be used as an example of the basic issue, of how we dare not be bound by any specific forms of expression, which are time-bound and quite foreign to the biblical and other ways of thinking. What, for example, would an East Indian or a Chinese who thinks quite differently do with this sort of thing? That there is something absolutely vital to the gospel at issue in the doctrine of the real presence as supported by the *communicatio idiomatum* is to be stoutly maintained. Really to deny what is intended in the *communicatio idiomatum* would be to deny

[3] See the 150 pages of F. Pieper, *Christian Dogmatics* II (St. Louis: Concordia, 1951), where the three genera are discussed in detail.

both the incarnation and the consummation of the creation in the resurrection and a new heaven and a new earth. It would in the end deny that man's flesh and blood and, indeed, the whole cosmos are to be taken up into the redemption. It would mean in the end a false "spiritualizing" of the gospel and the disastrous results of what we are reaping abundantly in the crass materialism of our day. With all the religious emphasis on the "spiritual" rather than the "material" men no longer know what it means to handle with holy awe and reverence the common elements of our daily life, the bread and wine of it, the earth itself and all its treasures, the sea and its myriad mysteries, all of which are to share in the eventual consummation. So theological students swill their food like swines at a trough so that they can rush back to their "higher spiritual pursuits," instead of making a joyful, sacramental occasion of the meal cf fellowship to which they have bidden the Lord Jesus to be the guest, in anticipation here, too, of their sitting down with him at the heavenly banquet tables. This is what is at stake in the *communicatio idiomatum,* but this must be released from the forms of expression in which it is imprisoned and must come to life, so that, without "splitting a gut" at this point we can recapture the "sacramental" character of all of life, in which God blesses us through sun and rain and food and drink and husband and wife and children, without any merit or worthiness in us. *This is by no means operating with a Roman Catholic conception of grace.* If this is not God encountering me in his gracious disposition, blessing me in spite of my unworthiness and sin, calling me to trust, thanksgiving, obedience, service, joy, then it is not the God of the Bible, the God in whom Luther believed, the God in whom I believe, God helping my unbelief.

This is a matter, as we have said, of a qualitatively different orientation being substituted and here the so-called existentialist categories will in our day render much better service.[4] At least this one point is made, there must be freedom to address the basic message

[4] See Jaroslav Pelikan, *From Luther to Kierkegaard* (St. Louis: Concordia, 1950).

of the gospel to our own day, in the thought-forms of our day, to take it, for example, to India and really to let it work itself out there as it meets the perennial problems of existence and not make the poor Indian talk like a German professor, neither Chemnitz nor Karl Barth nor Rudolf Bultmann (Martin Heidegger). The gospel is to mediate the living God and communciate an awareness of sin, grace, faith, and love in the uniquely Christian sense and not either a Western *Weltanschauung* or a sixteenth-century cosmology or a seventeenth-century theology.

It is possible to affirm, without thereby imprisoning yourself once more in a time-bound system, that neither life nor the gospel can be reduced to a system of thought, either doctrinal or philosophical. In the church, therefore, God himself is to meet man. This encounter, however, can take place only where the gospel is proclaimed and the sacraments are administered. Through these "means of grace" God imparts himself and this is not a communication of knowledge, but an "existential communication" in which to man in the totality of his existence the total God of creation, redemption, and sanctification imparts himself and with himself the peace and security and strength of this personal relationship. Nothing really passes directly from man to man, but through man's witness God imparts himself, as Barth would say, not horizontally but perpendicularly from above. This, however, needs the dialectical correction because this "direct from above," like all gifts from the "naked and transcendent" God, comes through the medium, *i.e.,* the brother who does the witnessing, the water and the bread and wine which accompany the proclamation. It is, of course, always this self-impartation of the living God which matters, but this cannot happen apart from the "pure" proclamation of the gospel, as it addresses man at the points of his absolute impotence. So all the crucial biblical words, sin, grace, faith, and so forth, are "known" and "understood" in their uniqueness only by those who have experienced that for which they stand. Who knows the God who is not the god of the philosophers but the Father of our Lord Jesus

Christ, except the one who has experienced him in the risen Christ in the power of the Spirit? And how shall he experience him except in the proclamation of the Word and the administration of the sacraments, that is, in the living fellowship of the church? (see Romans 10:14ff). Who knows what it means to be a sinner except the one who sees himself in the wrong orientation to the God of love encountered in Jesus Christ, and how shall he encounter this God if this God is not proclaimed? This kind of proclamation must address itself to the moment. It will make a tremendous difference whether the one addressed is a twentieth-century Marxian Communist, or a sophisticated aesthete, or star-eyed idealist, or a disillusioned, down-to-earth realist, or a Buddhist who has decided to take over where Christianity has failed.

OUTWARD FORM

If it is the gospel itself which is binding and gives freedom for constant restatement in meeting the needs of the moment, the same liberation applies to outward forms. The oneness of the church finds expression in the oneness of confession and proclamation in the kind of qualitative wholeness described and not in the uniformity of one centralized organization, oneness of administration, or constitution, or sameness of liturgical forms.

For this reason there has existed, even from the very beginning, a wide variety of church organization (congregational, presbyterial, episcopal), largely shaped, as were the first organized churches, after the model of existing institutions. The early churches followed both the Jewish pattern of the synagogue and the Roman pattern of institutional organization. State churches are a possibility, therefore, as well as free churches, though both must be held constantly under criticism and are legitimate only as long as the gospel proclamation is not interfered with. The American church organization was shaped by our democratic forms of government. There is nothing sacrosanct about it, and we must be constantly on guard against identifying the church and the American way of life at this point.

The only question that must always be asked is the central question concerning the gospel, the liberating and uniting act of God in Christ. Is this gospel not only unhampered but given the best possible full and free expression so that the body of Christ can really be and function and fulfil its mission? If the church should be persecuted and have to go underground, it might have to alter its organizational structure. This would not in the least detract from it as the body of Christ, if there were no longer the bishops and the prelates and all the hierarchy of ecclesiastical brass; in fact, it might be quite a long step in the right direction.

Here we are confronted with a new world, an urbanized world, a world of machines, of rapidly changing neighborhoods, where old patterns of organization and congregational life just do not fit. Yet we are bound by patterns made for stable societies which don't fit in an unstable apartment-house, mass-dwelling society. We are not free, as we ought to be free in the gospel, to adapt ourselves to this situation and to do the radically new and different thing which the moment requires. We must first move the colossus of ossified tradition and of intractable church administration. We, of all people, who have a doctrinal position which gives us the freedom to deal with this situation in a dynamic and explosive way, are precisely the most stolid and inflexible. "O foolish Galatians, who has bewitched you?" If we only would let ourselves be liberated, we would be free to go into the mission fields, both at home and abroad, walking only under the lordship of Christ, cut loose from false securities but anchored in the absolute security of the presence of the gracious God in Word and sacrament.

LITURGICAL FORMS—CHURCH ARCHITECTURE

So also the liturgy is not to be shaped by tradition only but rather by the understanding of the gospel itself as this has found expression also in tradition. No form, no matter how ancient or universal, should be preserved if it is not transparent to the gospel. This really requires separate treatment, in which the relation between bondage to the Reformation, *i.e.* to the gospel, and the freedom this bondage gives, is carefully worked out. It is clear, however, that it does not allow capricious playing around with gadgets and novelties in order to create mood and atmosphere. By the same token it rules out the reintroduction of elements, such as sanctuary lamps, sanctus bells, incense, and so forth, which have now come to possess a nonevangelical connotation. Roman Catholics have a right to resent this kind of poaching. The sanctuary lamp at the altar is a sign of the reserved host, and it is misleading to have the sign minus that which it signifies. This is an instance not covered by the freedom the gospel allows, because any rite or ceremony may when in controversy take on confessional character when under the circumstances its use means a compromise of the gospel. This basic endeavor should not be only to preserve what is best in the liturgical heritage. This is only a part of what is involved and there is no objection provided the criterion as to what is best is primarily the gospel itself. The basic concern must be for the gospel and man's response to it in worship, praise, service. Just as the gospel creates theology addressed to a situation, so also must the gospel be free to create liturgy which properly addresses the situation. The word "gospel" is in this context not to be deliberately given a subjective, revival-experience connotation, so as to create a cleavage between the so-called "catholic-objective" and "protestant-subjective" to begin with. There is nothing more catholic and objective than the gospel rightly proclaimed whether in sermon or liturgy or sacrament or the mutual consolation of brethren. No individual or committee therefore should have the unrestricted right of *imprimatur* on the worship of the church, whether official or unofficial. This would mean the direct reversal of the position of Article VII of the Augsburg Confession which makes agreement on the gospel and not agreement in rites and ceremonies decisive. What is said here about the liturgy applies also to church architecture where there should be the same freedom for the gospel to create houses of worship that express the gospel in a given situation.

FREEDOM IN PATTERNS OF CONGREGATIONAL PIETY

There must be freedom also in patterns of congregational piety. This deserves special consideration in view of American efforts at reunion. It refers not only to patterns of devotional exercise where there should be freedom in so far as this does not become a work-righteous individualistic self- or soul-nurture which contradicts the gospel; but it refers also to the actual exercise of piety, and to what is and what is not permitted good church members in matters of behavior (particularly such matters as smoking, drinking, card-playing, dancing, matters of dress, Sunday observance). We should first of all be aware of the fact that this is in large part a matter of social mores, geographically determined, and has very little to do with Christian faith. What is acceptable to a community in one part of the country is not acceptable in another. In some places it may be perfectly acceptable for a lady to sip a mint julep while no respectable lady would smoke, while in other places it is just the reverse. (In Denmark the sweet young thing smokes her big black cigar right down to the hilt.) A German pastor who in his native village was always the first to lead off in the dance together with his lady-love (his wife, of course) comes into a community where dancing is considered the prime instrument of Satan in sending innocents down the primose path.

It is not possible to find a solution to these problems of behavior on the basis of code-morality and the accompaning casuistry. The solution can come only from the center in the Christ who both liberates and unites. We have much to learn from those who take seriously the command, "Come ye out from among them and be ye separate!" Young peoples' meetings, complete with hip flasks and parked cars, which differ in no respect from secular groups and sometimes fall far below the high moral standards set by such secular groups, must re-examine themselves in the light of the gospel. Christians are to be in the world but not of it. But nonconformity to the world cannot be made obvious by a few arbitrarily chosen rules cut down to man's size. The paradigms of love given us in the Sermon on the Mount and in the life of Jesus himself as the second Adam must be taken quite seriously in their demand for absolute purity of heart, and we must recognize that there is no way of giving perfect outward expression to this singleness of purpose in seeking first the kingdom of God and his righteousness. We must take quite seriously the fact that we are always sinners and righteous simultaneously, always under both the judgment and the grace of God.

It has been the strength of the Lutheran Church not to confuse law and gospel, and Lutherans have been distinguished from other Protestants precisely at the point of the freedom which an evangelical ethic allows. Luther's explanation of the Ten Commandments needs to be grasped in its evangelical clarity. Accordingly the Christian life is a matter of the right relationship of fear, love, and trust in the God of deliverance ("I am the Lord thy God, who brought thee out of . . . the house of bondage, therefore thou shalt have no other gods before me"). There is in reality only one commandment, one absolute, that of trust in God out of which flows the *agape*-love of the neighbor. No obedience pleases God unless it flows spontaneously from a heart that rightly fears, loves, and trusts the God of deliverance. (Original sin consists in the lack of *vera metu* and *vera fiducia,* cf. Art. II, Augsburg Confession.) The instances cited in the commandments are, therefore, rather arbitrarily chosen instances of how love should show itself in specific instances.[5] The love-commandment is, therefore, by no means an eleventh commandment in addition to the others, but it is the one inclusive commandment. Yet the fact that Luther did not confuse law and gospel is quite apparent from his inclusion of the words which he moved from the beginning to the conclusion. God remains a jealous God, punishing the evildoer and rewarding those who do good. So there always remains the big-stick use of the law

[5] See M. Reu's address on Luther's Catechism at the 1929 Lutheran World Convention at Eisenach.

by which the sinner must be coerced. People, therefore, cannot be ruled by the gospel but only by the law so long as they remain *simul justus et peccator.* But this does not alter one whit the fact that the one law which is the criterion of all law is the "Thou shalt love," and for the Christian, in so far as he is the new man, there is only the love wherewith he is loved which has no regard for rewards or punishments. Here is an indicative and no longer an imperative, where the love of God flows in and through the Christian to the neighbor freely and spontaneously out of this right relationship.

UNITY IN DIVERSITY COMPATIBLE WITH LOVE

In crusading for the freedom which the gospel grants we should, however, not forget the other side. For the sake of love and peace every effort will, of course, be made to achieve as much uniformity as is possible without doing violence to conscience (I Corinthians 6:12; 10:23; 14:5, 12, 19, 33). This applies to organizational structure, liturgical forms, matters of conduct, and so forth. Uniformity can never in itself be redemptive. It must not be forced upon the conscience, but must be voluntarily accepted.[6] No rigid rules can therefore be set up. Circumstances will have to decide how much freedom there shall be in such matters. This "openness" to the new situations when they arise is part of what is meant by Christ both freeing and uniting. He does so in the moment, in the actual decision, in the life of the church; he does so existentially and not by a casuistry which has each case settled in advance on the basis of a code-morality. The preacher is not a lawyer, a scribe, well versed in the fine distinctions between what is lawful and what is not. Here is one of the prime distinctions between the evangelical pastor as a *Seelsorger* counseling in love, and the Roman Catholic priest making his fine distinctions between mortal and venial sins and parceling out penalties accordingly. The more difficult way is, of course, the way of love: "Owe no man anything but to love one

[6] See W. E. Garrison in *Third World Conference on Faith and Order,* p. 192.

another" (Romans 13:8), because the natural man will always prefer to be told precisely what to do and to leave undone at a level which remains under his control. The most difficult thing is to let go in faith.

THE ONGOING REFORMATION IN THE CHURCH

So we see clearly that we are engaged in an ongoing reformation. The Protestant principle is that we reserve the freedom to protest even against our own protest, subject to no norm except the gospel itself. The Reformation did not produce a perfect church which we need only to perpetuate or to which we need only to return every time we stray. There never was such a perfect church, not even in the primitive church, so it is not a matter of perpetuating or returning to that either. [7] The theology, the church practices, and so forth, of the Reformation are not in themselves normative for our day. Although the confessions are to be understood in the light of Luther's theology, that is, of his understanding of the gospel—or they will surely be misunderstood—Luther's theology is not to be apotheosized. No one of Luther's utterances is to be canonized. Luther said many things around the breakfast table which are highly interesting but scarcely bear canonization. What we must learn from Luther, therefore, is precisely his pointing away from his own word to the Word of God. What Luther and the Reformation did was to make clear the true and essential nature of the church and to provide a criterion by which the church should always judge itself to see whether or not it really is the church. Therefore both the freedom of the church and its unity, which bind it only to the gospel, forbid us to absolutize any historical form of the church, and any Lutheran church which does so is un-Lutheran and unconfessional, to say nothing of it being un-Christian. The gospel cannot be captured, imprisoned, safeguarded, guaranteed by any one ecclesiastical form which will preserve its purity and

[7] See *The Fulness of Christ,* p. 28.

power (II Corinthians 4:7), but the *dynamis* of the gospel will produce its own forms according to the needs of the moment.[8]

Every historical form of the church tends to autonomy; it tends to treasure its particular formulations and practices more than the gospel itself. We become more interested in perpetuating our notions than in proclaiming the gospel. What we have achieved and formulated is our own and we possess it, and so we are afraid to let go and give the gospel free reign—free reign even to correct and reform us.

Just as the individual must daily be reborn, so must the church. In her loyalty to the Reformation, the Lutheran Church must always re-examine her inheritance and judge her proclamation not by the Reformation but by that to which the Reformation points—the gospel, the Word of God, to which the Bible is the final, authoritative witness.

So the confessions are not absolute in themselves and exist only in protest to this kind of absolutization; they themselves deny it and they came into being in protest to this very kind of absolutizing of any human word. The confessions are *norma normata* and not *norma normans,* and derive their truth and validity from their conformity with the same gospel to which the Scriptures witness, by which norm and standard, according to the confessions themselves, all doctrines are to be judged. This disposes of the question as to whether the confessions are subscribed to "because" *(quia)* or "in so far as" *(quatenus)* they conform to God's word. Of course, so long as a person subscribes to the confessions he will do so on both counts, otherwise it is difficult to see how it can be an honest confession; but this dare never rule out the possibility of their nonconformity to the biblical witness. Whether or not this conformity exists remains always to be seen. Every generation, therefore, must by the confessions themselves be led back to the Bible to determine for itself what is and what is not harmony with the biblical witness. This is something no generation can do for another.

[8] See Report of Section on the Church, O. S. Tomkins, *op. cit.*

Every generation must, therefore, be on the constant lookout for the unevangelical elements in its tradition.

In the same way the Lutheran church must examine its relation to the other churches. We are no longer living in the sixteenth century, nor are we now in this mid-twentieth century any longer living in that heyday of liberalism which saw the near triumph of the so-called "modernistic" reinterpretation of Christianity. The denominations may no longer be actually holding to the same position they held in the sixteenth century. Indeed many are not, and, therefore, we must in honest conversation with them discover where they stand now and not at some time in the past. Then, to be sure, the same essential differences that divided the churches years ago may return. As previously stated, this has actually happened, and then the only hope lies in together driving to the center. "The way to the center is the way to unity."

THE QUESTION OF HERESY

The ongoing Reformation also requires the church to safeguard its proclamation and to deal honestly with heresy. The third World Conference on Faith and Order made a careful distinction between apostasy and heresy. It defined apostasy as "in essence a denial of the sole Lordship of Christ in profession, attitude or action" and urged individuals as well as denominations to be on constant guard against such denial.[9] Heresy, on the other hand is "defined as an error of doctrine persistently proclaimed against an established norm of the church, affecting vital matters of teaching." Since, however, life and thought, worship and action are inseparable, it involves a distortion of the spiritual life of the church and of the organic wholeness of the Christian faith. "It is agreed that there are *necessaria* (necessary articles) in the Christian faith and we would restrict the word 'heresy' to this sphere but we are not unanimous about their number and nature."[10]

[9] See Report of the Second Section on the Church, O. S. Tomkins, *op., cit.*, p. 250.
[10] O. S. Tomkins, *op., cit.*, pp. 29, 30.

The Lutheran Church's confessional position, as here interpreted, would make the criterion the gospel itself in its organic wholeness rather than a specifiable number of "necessary articles." The Lutheran Church likewise would reserve the right to safeguard its own ministry, and by excluding someone from its ministry it would not, therefore, pass a judgment that is reserved for God alone as to whether or not the man found guilty of teaching contrary to the gospel is or is not a Christian. It should concur with the position of Faith and Order, "In all these matters judgment should properly belong to the whole visible Church of Christ, but in our divided state this judgment can and must be exercised by individual denominations and even congregations, acting through all their parts, or, as others would say, orders. Every effort must be made pastorally and spiritually for the reconciliation of the offender. If, however, sentence must in the last resort be passed upon him, we are united in repudiating any recourse to secular coercion and violence."[11] The Lutheran confessional position would seem to me to provide the best safeguard against either too great laxity or too great narrowness in this matter, because it advocates being as broad and as narrow as the gospel itself. To make the charge of heresy stick, you really have to drive to what is central and not get hung up in a time-bound theology and varieties of forms of expression. You have to get behind these to the gospel itself. Above all you have to deal in true love and pastoral care with those who are believed to be deviating. This calls for serious self-examination as much as examination of the suspected offenders.

THE CONTINUITY OF THE CHURCH

The above emphasis upon openness to the moment raises the question of the continuity of the church. Karl Barth's dictum that the church never *is* statically, but only comes into being again from moment to moment needs to be balanced by the affirmation that there nevertheless is a continuity in the church: even as a line

[11] *Ibid.*, p. 30.

which consists of nothing but a succession of discrete points, nevertheless has a continuity, and even as the married life consists of more than a series of successive moments of endearment. As a man lives in the state of matrimony, so he is in the church in the covenant relationship.

It is not just a matter of asserting that the church is not always to change with the changing times and to be driven in every new direction by the changing words of doctrine, but is to preserve a constant witness. This, of course, it must do, preserving in changing formulations the one unchanging gospel. This is the indispensable mark of the church and therefore is essential to the continuity of the church. But there is involved something more than that, an actual, unbroken, historical continuity, not only of the message, but also of the people who constitute the church.

This is what the Lutheran Church has meant in the past by pointing to the objectivity of the means of grace, that is, the Word of God and the sacraments, in and through which God acts. Herein lies the real continuity of the church in this unbroken activity of God in the unbroken proclamation of the Word and administration of the sacraments. This is a succession, therefore, of the exercise of a function without which, of course, the church could not be. This function is, however, exercised in various ways, by the pastor in the church, the father in his household, and the brother consoling the brother. Hence there can on this view be no recognition of the episcopal succession as an essential mark of the church.[12]

Yet, in the body, there is a differentiation of functions and to this belongs the being sent out as an apostle, the right to preach publicly, and the oversight in the congregation. For this God will give the grace and strength necessary for the exercise of the function, as he will to all others in their vocation in their standing place *(Standort)*. And the authority that is recognized has the same

[12] See Newbigin, *The Reunion of the Church* (New York: Harper, 1948), pp. 178; 156-7; 168-9; 152-3.

divine sanction as that of the father in the home and the ruler in the state. If, therefore, also a pastor of pastors is required, this can be provided for without thereby capitulating to one structure (episcopal) only.[13]

No matter how signally one form of ministry may under certain circumstances have been blessed, there is nothing in the gospel which would so confine us. The gospel must remain free to create its own forms, and we cannot commit ourselves to something which the gospel itself does not clearly and unequivocally make essential. What we must allow is that there is to be authority in the church such as is required wherever people live together. This is nothing other than the recognition of the fact that government does not arise merely out of the human recognition of a need of a big stick to prevent chaos;[14] it does not just grow organically, but is God-given in order to serve his purpose of making it possible for people to live together in love.

Futhermore, there must be an office of the public proclamation of the Word and administration of the sacraments which is not simply usurped but which stems directly from God through the medium of the church itself. Christ wills the ministry because he wills the church. The very nature of the church is, however, violated by a self-perpetuating body of priests. This, with its denial of the priesthood of all believers, cuts to the heart of the gospel.

Finally, it can be recognized that pastors themselves need a pastor and also that God gives the grace, wisdom, and strength for the performance of a given task and will, in response to the prayer of the church, also furnish the ministry of the church with whatever grace is needed for the performance of its tasks. But to connect the bestowal of a special *charisma* with standing in the episcopal succession is false externalism.

All the above is compatible with the freedom of a variety of forms of organization for which we have pleaded. We must be

[13] Cf. I Cor. 3:21-23; 15:1-3; II Thess. 2:15; II Tim. 1:14; Rev. 3:10f).
[14] CF. Hobbes' and Rousseau's views on the origin of the state by means of contract.

consistent at this point if we are going to maintain our thesis and work out from the center.[15]

In conclusion there is the necessary eschatological reference. The common misconception that a belief in the imminent return of Christ leads to inaction and standing around on the street corners waiting for the moon to turn to blood needs the correction of showing how this faith in the glorious return really liberates for daring action. It is the this-worldly utopians who are the slaves of a determined process. For those who believe that the victory has already been won while the consummation lies yon-side the struggle in the turning from faith to sight, there is full freedom to walk under the lordship of Christ. It is this spirit that will most effectually release from the flight into false securities which a false clinging to tradition always represents.[16]

[15] See the quotation in *The Christian Hope and the Task of the Church,* pp. 27-28 from an article by Edmund Schlink in R. Newton Flew, *The Nature of the Church* (New York: Harper, 1952), p. 61.

[16] See Visser 't Hooft in *Third World Conference on Faith and Order, Lund, 1952,* p. 136.

V

Freed and United for Service in the World

It is high time that Lutherans, in deed as well as in word, make it clear that the doctrine of justification by grace alone does not lead to passivity. This is actually the heart of the gospel and the source and fountain of the new life in Christ. Far from leading to moral inertia and the disruption of community, it is the only basis on which there can be true life-together-in-love, true service of the neighbor which is something other than a veiled using of him for selfish ends. But then, of course, this doctrine must be understood not only in a narrow forensic sense but in the all-inclusive sense of man being straightened out in his relationship to God, himself, and the fellow-man, as we have tried to describe this. Then ethics is absolutely inseparable from dogmatics and we are here only spelling out a little more in detail the implications of the liberating and unifying act of God in Christ.

As a matter of fact the realization that this is the heart of the gospel certainly goes far beyond the confines of Lutheranism and is actually very often realized much better outside of the Lutheran Church than within it. This can be abundantly documented, and he who denies it is an ostrich with his head in the sands or else a proud Pharisee speaking thus and so within himself. This calls us to self-examination and repentance. If our practice has fallen below our proud profession, then in line with our thesis that it is the right proclamation that is crucial, there has been perhaps, after all, something wrong with our proclamation and our statement of the doctrine. This was the basis of Kierkegaard's attack on the church. Like Luther he did not try to reform the church by just flaying its practices. He attacked the theology which no longer required a radical transformation of life but allowed that every respectable burgher who was not in trouble with the police was a Christian and every well-paunched, child-begetting priest a martyr of the faith. So we, too, must ask ourselves again whether we are really centering on the center. Here now it shall become apparent whether or not the church is actually present in the right proclamation as the "hidden" life of love becomes recognizable in its fruits.

MAN'S EGOCENTRICITY AS DESTRUCTIVE OF COMMUNITY

It is man's egocentricity and his seeking of himself in others and even in God which cut to the very heart of the interpersonal relation and of life-together-in-love, as is revealed in the act of God's love in Christ, which is altogether for the sake of the beloved. As long as a person is using the other merely as a means to an end the personality of the other is being violated, raped. There are no better words than these to express exactly what is being done. If anything it is this using of the other which cuts to the heart of the interpersonal relation. In modern terms, this is reducing the I-Thou relation to an I-It relation.

It is not necessary to be a Christian to have this insight, up to a point. The philosopher Kant saw this clearly in his famous "categorical imperative," as opposed to all hypotheticals. There is to be no single "if"; no "I will do it *if, if* it profits me, or, *if* it will have this or that effect." Everyone must, without condition, treat everyone else as an end and never as a means. But true life-together-in-love is, nevertheless, not thereby attained, because this does not show how we are all actually dependent upon one another. This kind of an individual really stands in lordly isolation and self-sufficiency, not needing the neighbor. The human being, as Christianity conceives him, is, however, set down as a dependent being in the midst of community, where he owes his life to that God who is present to him in the masks of creation and serves him through the unique gifts of the parents, the neighbors and all those who contribute to his well-being by the vast variety of their gifts. An abstract egality of all men cuts as much to the heart of the Christian notion of life-together-in-love, where each serves the other with the peculiar gifts upon which the other is genuinely dependent, as does the natural egocentricity of man. In fact, this notion of egality is just another manifestation of the pride and egocentricity which destroy community. If all men are equal (in the sense of egality—with no real differentiation of function that makes them dependent upon each other), then they cannot be interdependent members of a body. Then the eye can indeed pour scorn upon the ear because it is not an eye and all members together pour scorn upon the head, especially the head, because each one has a head of his own. The interdependence in the Christian sense comes most clearly into focus when the sinner is dependent upon the word of forgiveness which the other brings, and to the one who is self-sufficient at this point it will always appear as a proud presumption that the Christian would make him dependent upon him. The sad story is that actually it often is a proud presumption on the part of the Christian, instead of it being the genuine service of love. All this we understand if we see how the proud Pharisees rejected Jesus while the humble of heart received him gladly.

FORGIVENESS ALONE LIBERATES FOR TRUE SERVICE

Let me restate this in an effort to show how the vicious circle of egocentricity must be broken if a man is really to be released for genuine service to the neighbor. This can only be done if a man is liberated in the right way by the assurance of God's love and forgiveness in the gospel and united with the neighbor in true life-together-in-love. Then it is not so that I may achieve either my own happiness or my own goodness or my eternal salvation, that I do any good deed whatever or that I serve the neighbor within the given structures of life. Let us try to see how destructive of all true goodness and how self-defeating the opposite procedure is. Let us suppose that I as a father have failed to provide for my family and their needs, not because I was the victim of circumstances beyond my control, but because I was wilfully self-indulgent and lazy and preferred my own pleasure to the sweat required if I were properly to provide for those dependent upon me and upon whom I in turn am dependent for the joy and happiness of my life. Now I could, by working harder tomorrow, make a certain kind of amends. An extra hundred dollars earned one week will cover the hundred dollars not earned the week before and so even the score. But can I in this way make amends for the lapse in my character, for the failure to meet an obligation, for the hurt of the wilful neglect? If I suppose that I can, then this is a corruption of morality.[1] It supposes that I can be better than really necessary and so accumulate a surplus of merit with which to cover a past fault. It also introduces an ulterior motive which destroys true morality. The good is now done not for its own sake or in order to help those who are in need but it is now done for my own sake, because I am anxious to keep my record clear. So I am really using others as a means to my selfish end, using them as a rag with which to wipe off the spots on the precious bib of my own self-righteousness. ". . . To make improving of our character the direct aim of our actions corrupts morality." [2] This leads eventually to frantic abuse of the neighbor and to heartless insistence upon "well-defined and manageable obligations," [3] which we have cut down to our size so as to ease our conscience, to make it possible to say that we have done all that can be expected of us, that we are righteous and not in need of forgiveness, and that when on occasion we are guilty of neglect we can make up for it by doing more on another occasion. This kind of quantitative manipulation

[1] I acknowledge my indebtedness in this whole treatment to J. Lesslie Newbigin, *Christian Freedom in the Modern World* (London: Student Christian Movement, 1937).
[2] Newbigin, *op. cit.*, p. 26.
[3] *Ibid.*, p. 25.

of "well-defined and manageable obligations" keeps us strictly in control and makes us intolerant of others.

How different is the whole situation where forgiveness for Christ's sake is at the center! The Christian lives in and out of a righteousness which is not his own but God's gift, Christ's righteousness covering his own unrighteousness. He is, therefore, never concerned to achieve righteousness or to make self-righteous amends for a past failure. All the past is covered by forgiveness and, therefore, he is now really open to the further and for real service to the neighbor in the place where God has put him (his *Beruf und Stand*—his vocation and standing place). So the husband and father will say to himself that he is as husband and father the recipient of certain gifts (however great or small they may be) upon which his wife and children depend and so he will serve them with these gifts for their sake. In so doing he realizes that he is a "mask" of the gracious God who has no other way of giving life and protection and other blessings to children, the weak, the dependent. This applies to each person in his *Beruf und Stand,* whether doctor, nurse, policeman, farmer, scientist, statesman, lawyer. The Christian serves in these areas not to achieve redemption —because this is the gift of God to him—but as the channel through which God's gifts flow to the neighbor. If it were not for the old Adam in all men this would result in true life-together-in-love.

When a man now fails in this *agape,* when, as in the above example, he wilfully, out of laziness and self-indulgence, fails to do what he should for his family, he can really close this chapter of his past and be open for the future. The sin is forgiven. I need not and cannot make amends for that, but here is the future with its present needs before me to which I can now wholeheartedly address myself, free from the burden of the past and any proud notions of making amends that are really rooted in selfishness and not in genuine concern for the neglected wife and children. Here now in this moment there are confronting me those needs which are indeed the result of my past neglect, but which need to be tackled now for their own sake and not as a sop to my pride. So I am free from the sin of the past, to address myself to the present need. This is Christian service out of gratitude for what has been done and in spontaneous love that meets the present need.

As the Christian is free from the past, so he is also free from the wrong kind of crippling concern for the future. Our times are in God's hands. I cannot by my frantic sweat and toil, even if I amass the fortunes of Croesus, build a sufficient bulwark against all the possible misfortunes of the future. I cannot in this way stave off death. So, although I must work hard and act circumspectly to the limit of my ability, it is never in these things that I put my trust, for "this night my soul may be required of me." In this way, also, I am freed for a service which is devoid of illusion and false security, and serves the purpose of the moment, not disdaining to make sensible provision for the future, but recognizing the basic insecurity of life and so getting the most out of what the present moment offers in simple trust and joy in God.

FREEDOM FROM CODE-MORALITY

The act of liberation and unification in Christ also frees in the right way from enslavement to a crippling code-morality. What is it that those outside the church criticize most often in church people? Is it that they see church people giving way in false freedom to their inclinations and "sinning that grace may abound"? Or, do they see how straitjacketed, repressed, and unhappy many Christians are by a confining, inelastic code morality, as though the sabbath were made for man and not man for the sabbath? Those who criticize traditional Christian morality with its arbitrary taboos and senseless inhibitions may be much closer to the New Testament than we allow. Jesus was to his contemporaries a glutton and a wine-bibber who did not hold the traditions of the elders, and Paul's greatest struggle was against those who wanted to re-enslave the people with the whole burden of circumcision. "Our peril is the reverse of antinomianism; it is pharisaism. We shall do well to listen to our critics."[4] When Christians bemoan the decay of moral standards it may be that they are only bemoaning the giving up of a tradition to which they themselves have grown accustomed and which they are falsely identifying with God's will. Those who protest against the absolutizing of relative moral standards in the name of the relativity of all moral judgments have a point. In the Scriptures there is only *one* absolute and that is God's will of holy love.

This is Kierkegaard's recognition of the fact that there is a stage beyond the universality of the ethical demand which we enter with a leap, where there is what he calls "the teleological suspension of the ethical" (not to be confused, however, with the Jesuitical principle that "the end justifies the means," because this is still on the level of the universal-ethical), where like Abraham we are under the direct command of the Lord, to do his will of love in that moment and let him cover in forgiveness, on the basis of the atoning suffering and death of Christ, the sin involved.

This is a matter of fields of personal relationships and not of universal laws and principles. In the Bible we see the distinction between rewards and punishments that issue directly in a chain of reactions from the deed itself, and obedience to the living God whose will is law. Punishments for sin are then viewed as the manifestation of God's wrath who gives man over to the consequences of his deed (Romans 1:18ff) in the same way that the believer sees himself delivered from judgment by the God who makes righteous (Romans 1:16-17). This is surrender to the lordship of God as Judge as well as Redeemer.

The freedom of the Christian, who is no longer under a code morality but under the command of God whose will is love, may be compared to that of the linebacker on a football team whose job it is to follow the opponents line-up, try to diagnose the offense, with freedom to throw himself in where he is needed, just so the

[4] Newbigin, *op. cit.*, p. 13.

ball is not advanced. He is not bound by the same rigid assignments as the other players, yet, of course, he too must play within the rules of the game and can't just do as he pleases. So the Christian's task is to keep the forces of evil from advancing, with freedom to maneuver, while nevertheless bound by the rules of the game which are the structures God himself has provided.

THE TWO REALMS OF GOD'S RULE

This requires clarification of the much-misunderstood and much-maligned notion of the two realms of God's rule in the world. If they are disjoined this leads to quietism on the part of the church which turns the world and its rule over to the devil. If they are falsely identified, law and gospel are confused and the gospel is turned into a program of world betterment. Here, again, a distinction *(Unterscheidung)* is to be made without causing a separation *(Scheidung Trennung.)*

First of all, there are not two separate kingdoms, the one ruled by Satan to whom God has abdicated, the other the church in which alone God remains Lord. It is better, therefore, to speak of the two realms of God's rule (or his left-hand rule and his right-hand rule) and the two corresponding realms of man's service. Moreover, the God who is Lord in both realms is the same God of holy love who, however, manifests his holy will of love in different ways, quite in accordance with what is in each case demanded. Finally, these two realms cut across each other so that the Christian always finds himself simultaneously in both realms, always under both the law and the gospel, even as he is *simul iustus et peccator,* in the home, the school, the playground, at work, in public as well as private life. In all these areas the Christian, who has experienced God's love and forgiveness, is nevertheless subject to rules and regulations, rewards and punishments. The child who disobeys in home or school is punished, the player on the football field is penalized, the preacher who does no work but relies on the Holy Spirit produces a "lousy" sermon and loses the respect of his hearers. The ruler whose order is not backed by force is soon overpowered by those who have no scruples about the use of force. Yet all these same people, if they are Christian, have also experienced God's grace and forgiveness and know that all their labors avail them nothing in the place of justification where God simply accepts them as they are and clothes them with a righteousness not their own.

This twofold rule of God results from the fact that not only does the world consist of the unregenerate and the regenerate but also each Christian remains divided within himself as the old man and the new man. So the Christian, who himself is divided, also lives in a divided world. In so far as he is the old Adam he is under the law and under God's left-hand rule, the realm of demand and of strict justice, the realm of force, of rewards and punishments; but in so far as he is the new man, he is free from the law and under God's right-hand rule, where strict justice, demand, rewards, punishments, and force have no place, because God's love has full and free course. The new man, therefore, holds all things in common with his brother and bears fully the other's burden; he accepts him unconditionally, shares with him his heart in genuine openness, uses no force against him, seeks no reward in serving him. He loves the brother in *agape* as he is loved. Yet he must do exactly what God does; he must deal with this person where he is and as he is, and this demands that the love itself may have to use stern measures.

This is the Christian's real predicament. He wants to put into full practice the so-called rigorous demands of the Sermon on the Mount—offer no resistance, turn the other cheek, give to the borrower, take no oath—and yet he finds he can't do it in this rough and tumble world. So, what is he to do—run away, or compromise his principles, or give up in despair? How can he take quite seriously the command that he is to remain in the world without being of it, that he is to remain in the calling wherein he is called, and manifest the new life there? How is he to be the salt of the earth and the light of the world?

THE DISTINCTION BETWEEN LAW AND GOSPEL

There is no help but to make the crucial distinction between law and gospel, between justice and love, and to see how God in his love has so structured the world that it is a place fit for the realization of his will and purpose which is life-together-in-love, and how the Christian living as the new creature in Christ revitalizes these structures.

What then is the crucial distinction between law and gospel? Law is what God demands. Gospel is what God gives. What is demanded and what is given is in each case the same, *viz.,* love, that is, genuine concern for the well-being of the other, regardless of his worth or merit, taking into account only his genuine need. The fulfilment of this law we find perfectly embodied in the second Adam who spent himself altogether for the sake of the beloved. It is the law that says *Thou shalt love,* and inasmuch as it is the law, it means business. It is God who demands this and, therefore, he calls to account those who do not conform, and he delivers them over to the consequences of the violation of this his will of love. Moreover, what God demands is that every law man makes, every institution he builds, shall serve the purposes of his love, by bringing men together in mutual helpfulness. To the degree that man's laws and institutions (his music, culture, art, education), really conform to the law of love they are the media in which God is present to men and imparts his blessings. He is present in these "masks" both in judgment and grace, in a genuine simultaneity.

THE GIVEN STRUCTURES OF THE WORLD

The structures are always there as something given, so that man is by his very creation set down in the midst of community. The sex differentiation in all its profundity rules out absolutely the self-sufficiency of man, for no life is given except through this union of one man and one woman. This establishes the monogamous family, as the order of creation, no matter how man may distort this, and as such it is more than just an order of *preservation (Erhaltungsordnung).* The family does not exist only so that children may be produced and protected, so that the gospel may be preached to them and their souls saved. This is really the Roman Catholic view which says that God created all souls at the beginning and now the game is to have as much copulation as possible and no birth control so as to give all these souls a chance to get out of the limbus, be baptized into the church, and so be saved. Hence even therapeutic abortions to save the mother are disallowed. To be sure the family exists for procreation and for protection, and the saving gospel is to be preached to every child born into the world, and in this sense the family is an order of preservation, but together with this the family is the kind of structure constructively fitted for the purpose which God intends right here and now. The same is true with respect to other structures, the state, the economic order, and the various cultural orders. God's house is like a house well-furnished for the kind of living God wants for his children. Here is the kitchen all fashioned for cooking, complete with all the gadgets, the dining-room, living-room, bedroom all in proper order.

The point is that these structures are decidedly more than just "orders of preservation." The state does not exist only so that the individual and the church may be protected so that souls may he saved. It serves a purpose also for this life and without by any means becoming a totalitarian or welfare state. The state is to make its positive contribution by providing the proper framework of order within which the other orders and the church too may function in order to bring men to the realization of the purpose for which they were created.

It is at this point that the distinction between the two realms becomes particularly apparent and important, and here the confusion of law and gospel must be avoided. The fact that sin has entered into the world must be taken into account. Since sin is a disturbed relation affecting the entire creation, God's method of dealing with it is also affected. Law is what God demands. Gospel is what God gives. God demands life-together-in-love and has as a gift of grace so structured the world as to make this a positive possibility. But because man is turned in upon himself and is not open both to give and to receive and also because he is ignorant and immature, it is necessary, if there is to be any life at all, to use force. Hence there is given to those in authority the power of the sword to restrain the evildoer and reward those who do good. This is God's left-hand rule, the so-called big-stick use of the law, and it is this which rules out ruling with the gospel (for this is a contradiction) or perfectly embodying the kingdom of God upon the earth. The antinomians believe they can dispense with the law and all live-together-in-love, as though sinful pride and egocentricity no longer exist. They confuse law and gospel. The opposite mistake, which equally confuses law and gospel, is made by all those who think that the kingdom of God can be brought in by force and that in the name of the Lord Christ you can wrest with force that which it is the gospel's alone to give—the kind of liberation and unification of which we have spoken. The sword, that is, the use of force, is therefore necessary as long as men are sinful but it can only keep order; it cannot really redeem; the law always accuses and never saves. In this sense the so-called "orders" belong to the sphere of the law.

So there is this area in which all men must take their place, toil and sweat, earn their reward, take their punishment, each in accordance with ability making his contribution to the needs of the community or else going hungry. Christian as well as non-Christian must pay his taxes, help protect against the marauder, perform the other civic duties which are imposed upon him. In this realm he cannot plead the kind of forgiveness of which the gospel assures him; he can only ask that all the extenuating circumstances be taken into account and that he get his due—no more and no less. This is the minimum. If there is more than that, if there should be forgiveness and consideration of real need regardless of worth, then it is because the power of love and the new age is breaking through. In one sense there is no difference between Christian and non-Christian in this matter of "civil righteousness." How good a chemist or governor of a state a man may be depends on the gifts he has and how well he applies them, and this he may do for any number of reasons besides the Christian motivation of love. He may be a good governor because he has a keen mind and imagination and is impelled by pride or ambition or humanitarian ideals, or he may be the best truck-driver on the highway simply because he has a simple one-track mind and is not distracted by idle day-dreams as he barrels his Bucephalus along the boulevard. And yet we simply cannot allow that it makes no difference whatever whether or not a man is a Christian and has become a new creature in Christ, whether or not the new age has actually begun and the liberation and unification in Christ actually taken place. To be sure there is a difference between the two realms, but we must now really take seriously that the new age has begun and try to spell out how a creative, constructive, liberating, uniting influence goes out from the one realm spilling over into the other. Luther is a safe guide here as elsewhere if only he is understood or, if really necessary, corrected and supplemented. He says in his explanation of the second petition of the Lord's Prayer that the kingdom of God comes indeed of itself without our prayer, but we pray in this petition that it may "come to us also," and then he goes on to state how this kingdom of God comes "When our heavenly Father gives us His Holy Spirit so that by His grace we believe His Holy Word, and live a godly life here in time and hereafter in eternity." Here is the clue. The Christian hears the Word of God's love (whether in church or at home or wherever) and there the "unknown God" whose heart he does not know, becomes for him the gracious God who accepts, forgives, abundantly blesses, and this is the God whom the Christian now takes with him into his daily life in the universal priesthood of which we have spoken. Whatever resources he has are thus put into the service of God that in and through them the world's needs be served.

HOW THEN DOES THE CHURCH RENDER ITS SERVICE IN THE WORLD?

So the Christian church renders its service in the world first of all through its proclamation of the gospel. The Quakers have a point when they mean to divorce their gifts completely from all proselytizing efforts, because the gift of love must have no strings attached. The gift should not carry the condition that you let your soul be harangued while you munch your coffee and doughnut in the warm shelter of the chapel. Christian missions have sometimes compromised themselves at this point. If a hospital is built or advice given on how to till the soil, then this should not be done as a snare in which to take the soul by surprise, but solely because this is the gift of love the moment requires and you have it to give. Of course, if you don't have it to give or someone else is already giving it, this settles it. Or when a person already has the well of Jacob from which the fathers drank and thirsted again, there is no point in multiplying pumps. Then is the time to supply that water of life so that they may never thirst again.

The proper dialectic must therefore be preserved. A church which restricts its mission to the silent service of love is no church. The church's primary task is the proclamation of God's Word, to convict the world of sin, to call to repentance, to warn against the judgment to come, to pour out the balm of Gilead. The church must call upon all who sit in the seats of the mighty and toy with human lives, experimenting with them as though they were chemicals in a tube, pushing them around like pawns, to face the claim of the Lord upon them. The church dare not tone down its witness or put it in the service of the status quo. Here is the Word of God that sent Amos to Bethel, Jeremiah to Jerusalem, John the Baptist before Herod, Jesus to drive the moneychangers out of the temple and to weep over his city. A word of judgment and a word of grace! But how difficult it is to know when to speak each word. Even the church gets in its own way and confuses its human desires with God's will. Yet from the clear and unequivocal word of love which knows no compromise we get a guidance more steady than that of the polestar above uncharted seas. So the church must sharpen the conscience of those who must make the decisions that affect the destiny of millions. It must call men to recognize wherein true humanity consists and condemn everything that does not conform to it.

The second means by which the power of the church breaks through from the one realm into the other is by means of prayer, prayer precisely for all those who do the world's work. The general prayers of our church are a wonderful example of what is involved. Futile as it may seem, prayer carries with it tremendous promise (I Timothy 2:1-4). The course of the world's events may be directed by the intercessory prayers of the faithful. There is no way of proving this; in faith, the church holds it to be so.

Thirdly, there is the very existence of the congregation itself in the midst of the world. What the church proclaims, it must also live, and for that for which it prays it must also work. The fountain of all true service in the world is in the life and worship of the congregation properly nurtured by Word and sacrament. There is to be the fellowship of the redeemed who demonstrate before the eyes of all the power of the new life in Christ. This calls for self-examination and more faithful use of the means of grace. Are we a church or a nice, comfortable club for the like-minded and like-heeled? Without trying to separate the wheat from the tares and remembering always that the church is for sinners, yet the salt is not to lose its savor and the city that is set on a hill is not to be hid (Matthew 5:13-16; Ephesians 3-10).

Finally there is the life of the individual Christian. This is the characteristic Lutheran emphasis, which, to be sure, has been distorted but has its justification. In the place where God has put him, with the gifts God has given him, in accordance with the needs of the moment, within the structures God has provided, the Christian is to render his priestly service. This is his stewardship or calling. Of course, we should recognize the primary meaning of "calling," called out of darkness into light by the gospel but, having been so called, we are also called to serve where we are. We have many "callings" in accordance with our several stations in life, as parents, children, students, workers, in each of which we are to strive to do God's will of love, meeting the demands of that situation, letting love take the form that time and place demand. So each one makes his contribution to the order, decency, humaneness, richness of life.

If there are things we cannot do alone, we must do them together. There must be concerted Christian social action in which Chrstians join for love's sake, provided only we do not thereby separate ourselves from others who share the same concern. Often it would be better to make common cause with all who share the concern and not ask questions about the motive. Thus it is with matters of better housing, juvenile delinquency, desegregation, civil rights.

SECULAR FREEDOM AND UNITY AS AN AID TO CHRISTIAN SERVICE

In a world divided such as ours, half-free, half-enslaved, we must face the problem of the relation between secular freedom and unity and the service rendered by the church. What of the countries in which the church has no real freedom to perform the tasks described, where to speak out boldly means persecution? Here the witness of the church inevitably brings suffering. The tension between church and world is much more clear and explicit. Under such circumstances the church as the wayfaring community gains real strength. It is purged of much chaff. It sees more clearly its real task and concentrates on it. The original significance of the martyr, who seals his witness with his life, returns. In a way it is easier to be a Christian under such circumstances, because the either-or is clear, and there is the challenge to which the human heart responds. This is the witness of thousands who confess with shining eyes that never did they experience the joy of the Christian life and of real *koinonia* (fellowship) with their Lord and each other as when all the trappings were stripped away and they had to face the real issues of life and death. Then they learned, on the yon-side of nothingness, when everything had been taken from them, what it really means to trust God and believe in the resurrection of the dead. They learned what it means to love and forgive the enemy who was brutually and ruthlessly oppressing them. They were really tried as by fire.

It is doubtful judgment indeed, therefore, which supposes that there is more fulness of life where the church enjoys the full freedom and protection of the state. It is much easier then to confuse the issues, to have the church become the servant of the state, to mistake good citizenship with being a Christian. This is our great temptation, and we must regard the secular freedom we have as a real burden of responsibility, because of the opportunities it provides and the extra care it demands. This is a stewardship of extra talents that makes exacting demands. From him to whom much is given much is demanded. And we must learn in the midst of these blessings to live as though we possessed them not. We must not make our service of God dependent upon the continued possession of these blessings. This would be to make of Christ the kind of earthly Messiah he refused to be. Then we'll be the first with the zealous to shout "Crucify him" when he refuses to be the champion of our liberties. To be freed from illusions like these is part of the liberty wherewith Christ has set us free.

CHRISTIAN PROCLAMATION AN AID TO SECULAR FREEDOM AND UNITY

On the other hand we would not be true to our calling, we

would not be taking seriously the coming of the new age and the fact that the whole creation is drawn into the redemption, if we did not strive in the right way to increase and distribute the blessings God has so richly provided. International peace, abundance of food, health, opportunity for education for all, all those things for which, for example, the United Nations stand, are not to be dismissed as a *fata morgana,* an ideal impossible of realization. It is not for us to set the limits. It is ours only to do what our hands find to do. We pray, "Give us this day our daily bread," and Luther includes here all that belongs to a truly human life. When we now see how in the midst of plenty life is crippled, then we cannot let the secular idealists outstrip us in our concern.

In this way Christian freedom and unity will serve as an aid to secular freedom and unity. The structures of grace that are already in the world, which I cannot see just as orders of preservation, but as contributing constructively to the life God wants, are strengthened by the presence of the church through the media described. The church does not set up programs to make the world better but it takes seriously Christ's promise that if we seek first the kingdom of God and his righteousness these other things will be added. Hence political, social, economical, cultural efforts ought not to be regarded as "messianic" and made into religious crusades. Yet the other side needs also to be stressed. This is God's world and the whole cosmos is drawn into the redemption. This is God's world and Lutherans of all people should not be afraid of this, but should be the first to say it. This is only working out the full implications of the sovereignty of love and the completeness of the redemption effected by Christ. This is not exchanging a theology of glory for a theology of the cross, for the people of God will remain the pilgrim people and will always have their cross to bear, precisely in their calling, until faith turns to sight.

I have purposely chosen not to treat the theme of "Free and United in Hope" separately because of the conviction that the eschatological perspective must pervade the entire Christian orientation. Eschatology is not something you can tack on at the end of the course as an afterthought, but it must pervade the whole. This is particularly true when speaking of the church's service to the world, because what the church does here will be determined by what it believes to be the ultimate outcome of history. If the kingdom is to be realized on this earth more or less Marxist style, then the church will react one way. If the ultimate outcome is only the salvaging of souls while the rest is scaffolding, you get another reaction. If the ultimate outcome is that the form of this earth shall pass away and that then the creation shall nevertheless be fulfilled in a new heaven and a new earth as the holy city comes down foursquare out of heaven shining with precious jewels, this will mean another quite different reaction. If salvation is inclusive, our concern must be inclusive. "The idea of a salvation that is a completed experience for each of us privately, apart from the consummation of all things, is a monstrous contradiction in terms." [5] Because the whole creation will share in the fulfilment we must handle the whole creation with the utmost reverence and dedicate it all to God's purpose, and build for eternity and not for time. This, of course, involves the risk of faith because only in faith is the victory won and the future secured.

Moreover, since the game of life is not like a football game when you can always figure out just how many minutes are still left to play, but is such that the final whistle may blow at any time, we should above all remember that what matters is not our grandiose plans and hopes for the future, but what we do now in this *kairos,* this present moment so big with opportunity and responsibility.

[5] J. Lesslie Newbigin, *Household of God* (New York: Friendship Press, 1953), p. 147.

Bibliography

THE LUTHERAN CHURCH IN THE UNITED STATES

The Distinctive Doctrines and Usages of the General Bodies of the Evangelical Lutheran Church in the United States. Philadelphia: Lutheran Publication Society, 1893.

Doctrinal Declarations—A Collection of Official Statements on the Doctrinal Position of the Various Lutheran Synods in America. St. Louis: Concordia, 1939.

The Common Confession, Parts I and II, Report of the Committee on Doctrinal Unity of the Lutheran Church—Missouri Synod and of the Committee on Fellowship of the American Lutheran Church.

United Testimony on Faith and Life, the Report of the Joint Union Committee to the Churches of the American Lutheran Conference.

Report on Lutheran World Federation, Issued by The Lutheran Church —Missouri Synod, 210 N. Broadway, St. Louis 2, Mo.

KRAUTH, C. P. *Theses on the Galesburg Declaration on Pulpit and Altar Fellowship.* Prepared by Order of the General Council, Philadelphia, 1877.

NEVE, J. L. *History of the Lutheran Church in America,* 3d rev. ed., Burlington, Iowa, Lutheran Literary Board, 1934.

NEVE, J. L. *The Lutherans in the Movement for Church Union.* Philadelphia, Lutheran Publication House, 1921.

———. *Die Galeburger Regel,* n.d., n.p.

LUTHERAN WORLD FEDERATION HISTORY, ETC.

BACHMANN, E. THEO. *Epic of Faith, The Background of the Second Assembly of the L. W. F.,* New York: National Lutheran Council, 1952.

LONG, RALPH H. *The National Lutheran Council, 1918-1938,* n.p., 1938.

The Lutheran World Convention, The Minutes, Addresses and Discussions of the Conference at Eisenach, Germany, Aug. 19-26, 1923. Philadelphia, United Lutheran Publication House, 1925.

The Second Lutheran World Convention, The Minutes, Addresses and Discussions of the Convention at Copenhagen, Denmark, 1929. Philadelphia, United Lutheran Publication House, 1930.

Proceedings of the Lutheran World Federation Assembly, Lund, 1947. Philadelphia, United Lutheran Publication House, 1948.

The Lutheran World Assembly, Lund, Sweden, 1947—A Summary Report. Philadelphia, United Lutheran Publication House, 1948.

The Proceedings of the Second Assembly of the Lutheran World Federation, Hannover, 1952. Geneva: Lutheran World Federation, 1952.

Fundamental Lectures at the Lutheran World Assembly, Hannover, 1952.

The Living Word in a Responsible Church: Study Documents for the Lutheran World Federation Assembly, Hannover, Germany, 1952. Geneva: 1952.

World Lutheranism of Today, A Tribute to Anders Nygren, Rock Island, Ill.: Augustana, 1950. See Aulen, Gustav, *The Catholicity of Lutheranism,* pp. 3 ff; Michelfelder, C. S., *World Lutheranism Today,* pp. 201 ff; Wentz, Abdel R., *Lutheran Churches and the Oecumenical Movement,* pp. 324 ff.

Christ Frees and Unites, Study Document, Third Assembly of the Lutheran World Federation. Geneva: 1957.

THE ECUMENICAL MOVEMENT

ALLISON, S. F. AND OTHERS. *The Fulness of Christ.* London: Society for Promoting Christian Knowledge, 1950.

BELL, G. K. A. *Documents on Christian Unity, three series.* London: Oxford, 1920-48.

Catholicity—A Study in the Conflict of Christian Tradition in the West —A report presented to the Archbishop of Canterbury. (Dacre Press) New York: Morehouse, 1947.

DREWETT, JOHN. *We Would Be One.* London: Highway Pr., 1954.

FLEU, R. NEWTON and DAVIES, RUPERT E. *The Catholicity of Protestantism,* being a report presented to His Grace The Archbishop of Canterbury by a group of Free Churchmen. Philadelphia: Muhlenberg, 1950.

FLEU, R. NEWTON, ed. *The Nature of the Church,* Papers presented to the Theol. Commission, appointed by the Continuation Committee of the World Conf. on Faith and Order. New York: Harper, 1952.

FORSYTH, P. T. *Congregationalism and Reunion.* London: Independent, 1952.

GENSICHEN, HANS W. *The Elements of Ecumenism.* Madras: Christian Literature Soc., 1954.

HANSON, ANTHONY. *The Meaning of Unity—A Study of a Biblical Theme.* London: Highway Pr., 1954.

HANSON, R. P. C. *The Summons to Unity.* London: Edinburgh House, 1954.

HOGG, WM. RICKEY. *Ecumenical Foundations. A History of the International Missionary Council and Its Nineteenth-Century Background.* New York: 1952.

JENKINS, DANIEL T. *The Nature of Catholicity.* London: Faber, 1942.

KENNEDY, JAMES W. *He That Gathereth:* A First Hand Account of the Third World Conference on Faith and Order. New York: World Council of Churches, 1952.

NEILLS, STEPHEN C. *Christian Partnership.* London: 1952.

ROBERTSON, E. H. *Account of the Third World Conference on Faith and Order, Lund, 1952.* London: SCM, 1953.

TOMKINS, OLIVER S., ed. *The Third World Conference on Faith and Order, Lund, 1952.* London: SCM, 1953.

The Christian Hope and the Task of the Church, Six Ec. Surveys and the Report of the Assembly by the Advisory Commission on the Main Theme, 1954. New York: Harper, 1954.

Faith and Order—The Report of the Third World Conference at Lund, Sweden, 1952. London: SCM, 1952.

World Council of Churches, First Assembly, Amsterdam, 1948: Man's Disorder and God's Design. New York: Harper, 1949.

THE CHURCH

BAILLIE, JOHN and MARSH, JOHN, eds. *Intercommunion; report . . . World Conference on Faith and Order.* Continuation Committee. Theological Commission. New York: Harper, 1952.

BERGENDOFF, C. J. I. *One, Holy, Catholic Apostolic Church,* Rock Island, Ill.: Augustana, 1954.

BRUNNER, E. *The Misunderstanding of the Church.* Philadelphia: Westminster, 1953.

DUNKERLEY, R., ed. *The Ministry and the Sacraments,* World Conference on Faith and Order. London: SCM, 1937.

MANSON, WM. *Church and Intercommunion;* some consideration bearing on the present problem. Edinburgh: 1951.

NEWBIGIN, J. E. LESSLIE. *The Household of God.* New York: Friendship, 1953.

———. *Christian Freedom in the Modern World.* London: SCM, 1937.

NILES, D. T. *That They May Have Life.* London: Lutterworth, 1952.

NYGREN, ANDERS. *Christ and His Church.* Philadelphia: Westminster, 1956.

NYGREN, ANDERS. *This is the Church.* Philadelphia: Muhlenberg, 1952.

PELIKAN, JAROSLAV. *From Luther to Kierkegaard.* St. Louis: Concordia, 1950.

THORNTON, L. S. *The Common Life and the Body of Christ.* London: Dacre, 1942.

———. *Christ and the Church.* London: Black, 1956.

World Conference on Faith and Order. Commission on Intercommunion. American Section. Washington (Conn.): 1942.

THE CHURCH OF SOUTH INDIA

The Constitution of the Church of South India. Madras: Christian Literature Society, 1952.

Doctrinal Statement Presenting the Confessional Basis for the Evangelical Lutheran Church in India. Vanigambadi: M.E.L.I.M., 1949.

HANSON, ANTHONY. *Should an Anglican Support the Church of South India?* London: Highway Pr., 1951.

NEWBIGIN, J. E. LESSLIE. *A South India Diary.* London: SCM, 1951.

———. *The Reunion of the Church, A Defense of the South India Scheme.* New York: Harper, 1948.

RAWLINSON, A. E. J. *The Church of South India.* London: Hodder & Stoughton, 1951.

SUNDKLER, BENGT. *The Church of South India, The Movement Towards Union, 1900-1947.* London: Lutterworth, 1954.

SWAVELY, C. H., ed. *The Lutheran Enterprise in India.* Madras: 1952.

WARD, MARCUS. *The Pilgrim Church, An Account of the First Five Years in the Life of the Church of South India.* London: Epworth, 1953.

LUTHER INTERPRETATION

WATSON, PHILIP. *Let God be God.* Philadelphia: Muhlenberg, 1948.

CARLSON, EDGAR. *The Reinterpretation of Luther.* Philadelphia: Muhlenberg, 1948.

RUPP, GORDON. *The Righteousness of God.* London: Hodder & Stoughton, 1953.

PRENTER, REGIN. *Spiritus Creator.* Philadelphia: Muhlenberg, 1950.

BAINTON, ROLAND. *Here I Stand.* New York: Abingdon, 1950.

KRAMM, HANS. *The Theology of Martin Luther.* London: Clarke, 1947.

ARTICLES

ALLEMANN, HERBERT C. "The Pittsburgh Agreement and Lutheran Unity." *Lutheran Church Quarterly,* XIII (1940), pp. 343 ff.

BERGENDOFF, CONRAD. "The True Unity of the Church," *Lutheran Church Quarterly,* XII (1939), pp. 270 ff.

DAVIS, H. GRADY. "Inspiration and the Pittsburgh Agreement," *Lutheran Church Quarterly,* XV (1942), pp. 154 ff.

FENDT, E. C. "The Theology of the Common Confession," *Lutheran Quarterly,* II (1950), pp. 312 ff.

HEINECKEN, MARTIN J. "Christ, the Christ, Alone Frees and Unites," *Lutheran World,* Supplement 1, 1956.

JACOBS, C. M. "The Washington Declaration—An Interpretation," *The Lutheran Church Review,* XL (January, 1921).

NYGREN, ANDERS. "The Basis of Ecumenicity in Lutheran Theology," *The Lutheran World Review,* I (January, 1949), pp. 15 ff.

SCHMAUK, THEO. E. "The Principles of Cooperation and Fellowship, 1907; Selections from Reports to General Council," *The Lutheran Church Review,* XXXIX (1920), pp. 169 ff.

SUESS, THEOBALD. "The Question of Intercommunion," *The Lutheran World Review,* I (January, 1949), p. 23 ff.

VALENTINE, M. "The 'Fundamental Principles' of the General Council," reprinted from *The Lutheran Quarterly,* October, 1887.

VISSER 'T HOOFT, W. A. "The Issues to be Faced at Evanston," *The Chicago Theological Seminary Register,* January, 1954, pp. 7 ff.

"Federation of Evangelical Lutheran Churches in India—Doctrinal Statement," *Lutheran World Review,* II (1950), 222-238.

"A Symposium on the Baltimore Declaration," *Lutheran Church Quarterly,* XII (1939), pp. 279ff.

I. "An Interpretation of the Baltimore Declaration," by H. Offermann,

II. "Implications of the Baltimore Declaration for Dogmatics," by Emil C. Fischer.

III. "Implications of the Baltimore Declaration for Christian Education," by O. Fred. Nolde.

VAJTA VILMOS. "The Problem of Church Union in South India," *Lutheran World,* September, 1956, pp. 110 ff.

Type used in this book
Body 11 on 13 Garamond
Display, Garamond
Paper: RRR Standard White Antique